EAST COOPER GAZETTEER

EAST COOPER GAZETTEER

People, Places, and Events in History

SUZANNAH SMITH MILES

Charleston London

History
PRESS

Other local history books by Suzannah Smith Miles:

The Beach
Island of History: Sullivan's Island from 1670–1860
Time and Tides on the Long Island: Isle of Palms History, Flora and Fauna
The Sewee, Island People of the Carolina Coast
Scoundrels, Heroes & the Lowcountry Outdoors
Writings of the Islands
Writings of the Lowcountry

Published by The History Press
18 Percy Street
Charleston, SC 29403
866.223.5778
www.historypress.net

First published 2004

Manufactured in the United Kingdom

ISBN: 1-59629-002-1

Library of Congress CIP data applied for.

CONTENTS

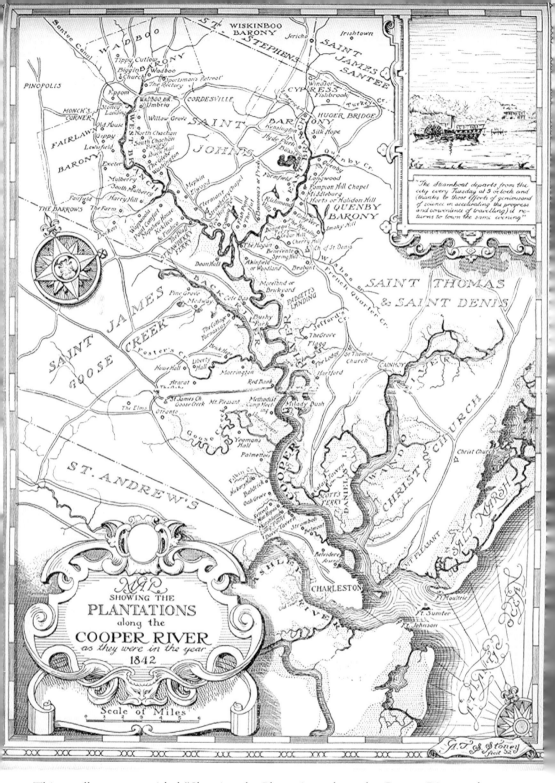

This excellent map entitled "Showing the Plantations along the Cooper River as they were in the year 1842" by A.T.S. Stoney, appeared in the 1932 edition of John B. Irving's *A Day on Cooper River*.

Author's Note

A GAZETTEER, BY DEFINITION, IS A short, encyclopedic listing of information in alphabetical order. By no means should this work be considered a complete history of the East Cooper area. Instead, this edited and hopefully improved version of my original gazetteer, first released in 1993, is designed to serve as a concise introduction to some of the people, places, and events that have shaped this area's past and present.

The East Cooper population has grown dramatically since the first *Gazetteer* was published. Daniel Island, Cainhoy, and lands on Highway 17 North towards Awendaw were still "hinterlands" 11 years ago. This revised gazetteer now incorporates these areas as well as McClellanville and the Santee Delta.

The information was drawn from numerous primary and secondary sources. For simplification, they are not footnoted in the text but shown in a bibliography. Hopefully, the information is presented in an easily accessible format. When a name or place is written in capital letters within the text, this denotes a separate entry elsewhere in the gazetteer. For instance, "Boone Hall" is cross-referenced with "Brickmaking."

I have also shortened the titles of various newspapers quoted; for instance, the *South-Carolina Gazette*, which went through numerous name changes during its periods of publication, is simply referred to as *Gazette*. Likewise, the *News & Courier* is shortened to *Courier*; "The Parish of St. Thomas & St. Denis Parish", I refer to as "St. Thomas Parish."

I have standardized the spelling of the Indian tribe as *Sewee*, although it is often found spelled as *Seewee* in historical texts. Both spellings are appropriate.

And lest you think my own spelling is flawed, remember that passages set off by quotation marks are direct quotes. Spelling in earlier times was not yet standardized and writers were creative in the ways they spelled both names and words. I have left their writings intact.

Hopefully, I have come as close as possible when presenting dates since calendar changes and sources often conflict. My apologies, particularly to descendants of people I have noted, if my genealogical information is inconsistent with theirs. Genealogies are invariably conflicting and difficult to pin down.

My sincere thanks to the staff at the Charleston Library Society and at the South Carolina Room of the Charleston Public Library for their always cheerful support. And finally, a very special thanks to Mary-Julia Royall, author and historian, for so gladly sharing her vast knowledge of both the history and the people of the East Cooper area. She is the East Cooper's true historian, a good friend, and, above all, a grand lady.

Suzannah Smith Miles
2004

A Concise History

Upon consideration . . . of the better disposing of people that hereafter shall arrive in this place . . . it is advised
and resolved . . . that Captain John Godfrey, Captain Thomas Gray, Mr. Stephen Bull, Mr. Maurice Mathews
and Mr. Christopher Portman do with what convenient speed they may, go and view all the places on this River and
Wando River and take notice . . . of what places may be most convenient to situate Townes upon.

Journals of the Grand Council
October 24, 1671

Fifty million years ago, when the great ice caps rimming the globe began to melt, the oceans rose and covered the land. The Carolina shoreline was then far inland, creating tall beach dunes known as the sand hills of Carolina that, today, form a line through the center of the state. It was during this prehistoric period that mammals began to replace the great reptiles that had previously stalked the earth. Vegetation became more specialized with the beginnings of deciduous trees and shrubs. The bony fishes appeared.

Finally, the sea receded. As the land stabilized, rivers and inlets carved their way seaward and the coastal barrier islands began to form. Colossal mastodons and giant sloths, saber-toothed tigers and small, dog-sized horses roamed the new, emerging coastline. Massive garfish and behemoth sharks ruled the sea; alligators stalked the swamps. Clams and other shellfish lined the riverbeds and the land east of the Cooper River began to take its present shape.

Looking out over today's manicured lawns and tree-lined avenues, it is difficult to imagine this as the same land where mastodons once reigned. Yet from prehistory to the present, this land has provided sanctuary and sustenance for both man and beast.

 ## The Indians

At the time of European occupation, there were an estimated 19 different tribes of Native Americans living along the Carolina coast. These were a generally peaceful people who lived in small villages along the creeks and rivers that would retain their names. Charleston harbor formed a natural dividing line between the tribes of the upper and lower coasts. From the harbor southward were numerous tribes that came to be known as the coastal Cusabo, primarily members of the Muskhogean and Algonkian linguistic groups. These included the Etiwan on the Wando River, the Kiawah on the Cooper River, and, to the south, the Stono, Edisto, Ashepoo, Combahee, Wimbee, and Coosa. From the harbor north, they were generally of the Siouan linguistic group, including the Sewee and Santee.

The tribes living east of the Cooper River at the time of European settlement were the Wando near the mouth of the harbor, the Etiwan near the junction of the Cooper and Wando Rivers (now Daniel Island), and the Sewee, who generally dominated the area between Copahee Sound and the Santee River.

Despite linguistic differences, the customs and lifestyle of the coastal tribes were remarkably similar. They lived within a sophisticated social and political structure, with each tribal unit governed by a king, or cassique, under which an assembly of tribal leaders, often including women, managed the laws and affairs of the people. Their religion was pantheistic and, like the ancient Greeks, they worshipped a number of different gods who they believed controlled the environment around them. Resourceful and independent, they gleaned everything they needed from the woods, the sea, and the soil. They were proficient hunters and fishermen and also farmed small plots where they grew gourds, melons, and corn. For necessities not found locally, they traded with tribes from the north and inland.

Many of today's major roadways were once Indian trading paths. Georgetown Road, once the old stage route and now generally Highway 17 North, was built on the Sewee Broad Path, a trail that ultimately led all the way to upstate New York. Likewise King Street on peninsular Charleston was a Broad Path that went all the way to the Mississippi River.

Their houses were round or oval and made from a bentwood frame covered with moss, palmetto fronds, and bark. They roasted their game on poles over a fire and made bread from ground acorns and other nuts. They created pots and cooking utensils of fired pottery elaborately decorated with swirls and figures.

By far, deer was their most important animal. Venison provided food and the deer's hide was used for clothing and blankets. Sinew and entrails became thread, fishing line, and rope. Deer horn was boiled to make a form of glue, while the tips of horns were used as arrow points. Even the brain of the deer was used in the tanning process, at which they were expert.

Almost as important was the bear. From birth, they constantly coated themselves with bear fat mixed with the juice of the bloodroot plant which tinted their skin into a dark ruddy complexion, perhaps the source of the sobriquet, "redskin." Bearskin made robes, bed coverings, and moccasins. They harvested crabs and shellfish for food and ornamented themselves with jewelry made of shells. Conch shells were used as cooking and drinking utensils; a conch shell on a handle made a useful hoe. Other shells, like the razor clam, were used for shaving and skinning hides.

This dignified coexistence with the land was forever ended with the coming of the white man. Despite their natural healthfulness, the Indians had no immunities to the diseases brought from Europe and later, Africa. Smallpox roared through villages, sometimes completely eradicating an entire tribe. With the introduction of rum, a more insidious disease—alcoholism—reaped tragic consequences.

Despite its illegality, in the late 1600s there began a period of illicit trade in Indian slaves, perpetuated by less than honorable colonists and Indians alike. Hundreds, possibly thousands, of Indians were taken as slaves and sold to Caribbean sugar plantations, where they immediately died. Finally, war, particularly the Yemassee War of 1712–1715, claimed untold numbers.

It is estimated that from disease, the effects of rum, the illicit slave trade, and war, the population of the coastal tribes dwindled from an estimated 3,000 people in 1600 to just over 500 by the early 1700s.

 Colonial Settlement

In early March 1670, the ship *Carolina*, after an arduous crossing from England, finally made landfall on the Carolina coast. Their landing place was on the northeast point of Bull's Island overlooking the wide expanse of Bull's Bay and Cape Romain.

They had been aboard ship for over three months, suffering seasickness, water shortages and repeated storms and hurricanes. Seeing this strange land that lay before them—a wild, savage land of impenetrable woods, expansive marshes, and windswept islands—must have been simultaneously exhilarating and frightening. As the ship drew near, they were heralded by a group of Indians, likely a Sewee hunting party, shouting and waving to them, motioning the best spot to bring a longboat ashore.

The Sewee knew Bull's Island as *Onesicau*, the largest of their hunting islands, the barrier islands that stretched from Charleston to Bull's Bay. The remarkable welcome they gave the arriving colonists was described by one of the ship's passengers, Nicholas Carteret:

. . . ye Longe boat went Ashore . . . upon its approach . . . were ye natives who upon ye Strand made fires & came towards us whooping in theire own tone and manner and making signes also where we should best Land, & when we came a shore they stroaked us on ye shoulders with hands saying Bony Conraro Angles [good friends, Englishmen], *knowing us to be English by our Collours (as we supposed) we then gave them Brass rings & tobacco at which they seemed well pleased . . .*

. . . as we drew near to ye shore A good number of Indians appeared clad with deare skins having with them their bows & Arrows, but our Indian calling out Appada [their word for 'peace'] *they withdrew & lodged theire bows and returning ran up to ye middle in mire and watter to carry us a shoare where when we came they gave us ye stroaking Complim't of ye country and brought deare skins some raw drest to trade with us for which we gave them knives beads & tobacco . . .*

A few days later a party from the *Carolina* were invited to a main village of the Sewee. Likely near what is now the community of Awendaw, they entered the "Hutt Palace" of the tribal leader:

. . . who meeting us tooke ye Governor [William Sayle of Bermuda] *on his shoulders & carryed him into ye house in token of his chearfull Entertainment. Here we had nutts & root cakes such as their women useily make . . . & watter to drink for they use no other lickquor as I can Learne . . . While we were here his Ma'tyes three daughters entred the Pallace all in new roabs of new mosse which they are never beholding to ye Taylor to trim up, with plenty of beads of diverse Collours about their necks; I could not imagine that ye savages would so well deport themselves . . . who coming in according to their age & all to sallute the strangers, stroaking of them.*

It had been the colonists' original plan to settle further south at Port Royal, near present-day Beaufort, where previous European settlements had been attempted. The Sewee, enjoined by the Kiawah, persuaded the colonists to instead establish their town on a safe, high spot on the banks of the Ashley River. This first settlement was named Albemarle Point and is now Charles Towne Landing. In 1680, they moved the town to its present site on the peninsula between the Ashley and Cooper Rivers, naming it Charles Town in honor of the reigning British monarch, Charles II.

It has been said that the Carolina settlement was "an extraordinary scheme of forming an aristocratic government of a colony of adventurers in the wild woods, among savages and wild beasts." The Carolina colony was, by and large, an experimental extension of the English colonial effort in the Caribbean islands, particularly the island of Barbados. It was a planter from Barbados, Sir John Colleton, who first suggested to Lord Anthony Ashley Cooper that they pursue the establishment of a colony in that "rich and fertile Province of Carolina." It was also from Barbados that the initial explorations of the Carolina coast were made, first by Captain William Hilton in 1663 and by Robert Sandford in 1666.

Barbadian immigrants quickly comprised a majority of the initial population of the colony. Ultimately, the Barbados system provided the standard by which the colony's political, social, and religious structures were based.

Overseeing the settlement of Charles Town were eight Lords Proprietors, men who had been given the land called "Carolina" by Charles II for their support in helping the monarch regain the throne. Initially, the colony was to have two classes of nobility, Landgraves and Cassiques, who, as in England, were to serve as the lords of the land. Each Landgrave was to receive a barony of 48,000 acres; each Cassique, 24,000 acres.

For others, land was granted through the head right system, which automatically allotted a certain amount of acreage as arrival rights to each man coming into the colony. The size of the grant depended upon how many people he brought into the colony. These included members of his family, indentured servants, and slaves.

The original baronial design for the colony was tempered by the remarkably democratic Fundamental Constitutions of Carolina, written by Lord Ashley with celebrated philosopher John Locke. This document outlined the governmental policies for the Carolina settlement and provided for a colonial governor, a grand council, and an elected parliament. It also allowed an uncommon guarantee in the 17th century—the right to worship in the religion of one's choice.

Consequently, a significant number of colonists came for religious reasons, including large numbers of French Protestants called Huguenots who had been forced to flee their native country. There were also a small but significant number of Quakers. In large numbers came Presbyterians and Congregationalists, also known as Dissenters since they "dissented" with many of the practices of the established Church of England.

Grants for East Cooper lands began almost immediately following the settlement at Albemarle Point. The first land grant for Daniel Island, then called Ittiwan Island, was in 1671; by 1679, lands were being granted on the East Branch of the Cooper River. Captain Florence O'Sullivan received a grant for the area we know today as Mount Pleasant's "old village" and, in 1674, was given charge of a "great gunn" on the harbor island that would eventually carry his name. From Barbados came Colonel John Godfrey Sr., one of the first to take up lands near Shem Creek. Likewise, David Maybank and George Dearsley began taking out warrants for land at Hobcaw, marking the beginning of what is considered the first shipyard in America.

Between 1680 and 1688, an estimated 450 French Huguenots arrived in the colony establishing French Santee at Jamestown on the Santee River and the French Quarter on the Cooper River's East Branch.

In 1695, a group of 52 Congregationalists from Ipswich, Massachusetts, arrived in the colony at the instigation of the Quaker governor John Archdale. Allotted lands between the Wando River and Sewee Bay in the area known as Wappetaw, they built perhaps the first house of worship east of the Cooper, the

Wappetaw Meeting House. At about the same time, either part of their group or a second group from Massachusetts settled on the Cainhoy peninsula.

By the early 1700s, large plantations fronted almost all the land along the rivers. Rice was the favored crop and the tidally influenced but freshwater rivers provided a way to flood and drain the fields as needed. On high ground, subsistence food crops were grown and livestock raised. Lumber was a lucrative commodity, serving both the shipbuilders and the Charleston market. In the 1740s, indigo became a second money producer for the rice planter. Planters on the Wando and Cooper Rivers also discovered another "crop" beneath the soil, a rich vein of red clay. Soon, brickmaking concerns lined the rivers, adding even more money to the plantation economy.

These plantations needed a sizable labor force. Indentured servants came from the British Isles and Europe, while the slaves brought from Africa—some 2,400 imported annually by the 1730s—soon led to a solid black majority.

All major business was conducted in Charles Town, and most plantation owners had houses in the city. Since roads were few and land travel was difficult, travel between plantation and town was primarily by boat. In 1700, Captain Anthony Mathews established the first ferry connecting Hobcaw and Charles Town. Soon a ferry across the Wando River at Cainhoy followed, and on the East Branch, the Bonneau Ferry. At the new town called Childsbury, the Strawberry Ferry crossed the Cooper River's West Branch.

In 1706, the passage of the Church Act separated all of the lands in South Carolina into parishes, designed as both political and religious entities. Christ Church Parish encompassed the land area from the harbor to Wappetaw; St. Thomas Parish served Daniel Island, Cainhoy, and the settlements on the East Branch. The upper Cooper and its West Branch were served by lower St. John's Parish, Berkeley, with the church at Biggin serving as the parish church. St. James Santee served the South Santee plantations.

 ## A Town Emerges

In 1749, wealthy Charleston merchant and statesman Jacob Motte purchased land on what was then called Hog Island Hill, just to the south of Shem Creek. Named Mount Pleasant Plantation, the site's original purpose may have been as a summering place. Like other plantation owners who were beginning to build summer houses on the waterfront, Motte may have been seeking a place to escape the heat of the summer and the diseases that accompanied warm weather in the swampy lowlands.

Mount Pleasant's close proximity to Charles Town made it particularly favorable for settlement. In the early 1760s, Englishman Jonathan Scott purchased 100 acres adjoining Mount Pleasant Plantation and began to develop it in the fashion of a typical English village. Called Greenwich Village, it was designed with town lots overlooking the harbor and had a town common for firewood.

In 1770, James Hibben purchased Mount Pleasant Plantation from Motte's estate and Hibben's Ferry soon connected the village area with town. Shem Creek was burgeoning with activity for businesses that found this accessible, deepwater creek advantageous. In the 1740s, Peter Villepontoux had a lime kiln on the creek to support the nearby brickyards. In 1795, inventor and millwright Jonathan Lucas established the first water-driven, combination rice and saw mill on the creek. The adjoining lands came to be known as Lucasville.

In 1819, Moultrieville on Sullivan's Island was incorporated, with the island becoming one of the most popular summer resorts on the eastern seaboard. In the Mount Pleasant village area, there was a new development to the north of town called Hilliardsville. There was the addition of a second ferry dock and excursionists came regularly from Charleston to Mount Pleasant to enjoy the salubrious air or one of the many balls and entertainments held at the newly built Alhambra Hall. A diversity of literary, musical, and agricultural societies commanded the social scene. Scientific achievements abounded, and naturalists such as John James Audubon were regular visitors. Finally the area had grown in such size and number that, in 1837, the various villages united and, taking the name of Mount Pleasant, the town was born.

The Civil War and Reconstruction changed forever the prosperity of the antebellum plantation society. The war left the country in ruins—the former social, political, and economic structure destroyed. Many of the plantations had been plundered and the houses burned. The fields lay fallow. Of the many brickyards on the Wando and Cooper Rivers, only the one at Boone Hall was strong enough to survive the post-war depression. A series of back-to-back hurricanes in the late 1800s and early 1900s destroyed the fields of the few plantations that had attempted to grow rice after the war.

Recovery was slow and, for some plantations, there would be no resumption of activity. On others, truck farming replaced rice and cotton, while phosphate mining brought a welcome prosperity to some in the late 1800s. In the 1920s and 1930s, the Cooper and Santee River rice plantations became hunting retreats for wealthy northerners, the former rice fields ideal for duck hunting. Other places slowly reverted back to their primeval wildness.

In 1898, an enterprising Charlestonian, J.S. Lawrence, saw a new economic opportunity on the then uninhabited island just north of Sullivan's Island. Long Island was renamed "Isle of Palms" and in less than two years it was a resort rivaling Atlantic City in popularity. This endeavor not only introduced additional ferry service from Charleston, but an electric trolley line was built to take passengers from Mount Pleasant to this island resort. A new bridge was built over The Cove from Mount Pleasant to Sullivan's Island. For the first time a bridge also spanned Breach Inlet.

On Sullivan's Island, the posh New Brighton Hotel was entertaining guests with its bathing houses and boardwalk. With World War I, Fort Moultrie was activated to a never-before-seen strength. The economy of the area was no longer agriculturally driven, but dependent upon the military, tourism, and the shrimping and fishing industry that had begun to flourish on Shem Creek and in McClellanville.

With the opening of the Cooper River Bridge in 1929, the area was finally linked by roadway to Charleston. The rest, as they say, is history.

The once-great plantations are now impeccably groomed neighborhoods and subdivisions. The islands are no longer summer resorts, but year-round communities. Yet despite the change, the area still retains a unique pride of place, a remarkable sense of history. This history is not only physically preserved at places such as Boone Hall, Snee Farm, and Fort Moultrie, it is held in the hearts and minds of those who live here. The people, places, and events of the past remain part of the everyday continuum, guideposts for the area's future.

The Gazetteer

ABCAW – Alternate spelling for HOBCAW, a Siouan word meaning "elevated way." (See HOBCAW)

ABOVE THE SALTS – Also referred to as "the freshes," the 18th-century term for the area of the rivers beyond the salinity point. Captains of vessels awaiting goods were careful not to leave their ships anchored in the harbor too long because of the quick damage salt water marine worms could do to a ship's hull. The upper reaches of the ASHLEY, COOPER, and WANDO Rivers were used as anchorages, particularly in the summer months when shipping from Charleston was slow since RICE was harvested in the fall.

ADDISON'S BRICKYARD – DANIEL ISLAND brickyard located on the west bank of BERESFORD CREEK. Thomas Addison had a thriving brickyard here between 1751 and 1776.

ADDISON'S SHIPYARD – Various shipyards were located on SHEM CREEK starting in the early 1700s. Addison's Shipyard was there in the 1860s.

AGASSIZ, DR. JEAN LOUIS RUDOLPHE (1807–1873) – Internationally acclaimed doctor and scientist noted for his simplification of Linnaeus' method for cataloguing specimens. In 1851, Agassiz assumed a professorship at the Medical College of Charleston. He also established a SEASIDE LABORATORY on SULLIVAN'S ISLAND to study marine plants and fishes. With his previous research in South America and on the northeast Atlantic coast, the Sullivan's Island laboratory allowed him to complete the first full scientific study of marine life of the entire Atlantic shoreline. (see JOHN BACHMAN, RAVENEL, SEASIDE LABORATORY)

AHAGAN – Area on the Cooper River's EAST BRANCH just to the west of FRENCH QUARTER CREEK. The name is undoubtedly of Indian origin, meaning unknown. It became known as the RICE plantation called the HAGAN. Ahagan Bluff is first mentioned in a grant to Samuel Wilson in 1688 for 1,000 acres "on a gently rising hill, viz. Ahagan Bluff." In 1722, the plantation was owned by WILLIAM RHETT; in 1748, by Daniel HUGER. (see EAST BRANCH)

ALBEMARLE – The smallest of the three ships which brought the original English colonists to CAROLINA in 1670. Mastered by Edward Baxter, she was a two-masted sloop, or shallop, weighed 30 tons, and sailed with a five-man crew. On November 2, 1669, the *Albemarle* was driven ashore by a hurricane at BARBADOS and lost. Passengers and crew continued their journey on the *Three Brothers*. (see *CAROLINA*)

ALBEMARLE POINT – Now Charles Towne Landing, this site on the ASHLEY RIVER was the original settlement of the Charleston colony in 1670. The name honored Lords Proprietor George Monk, Duke of Albemarle.

ALHAMBRA HALL – A town park and clubhouse in the OLD VILLAGE of MOUNT PLEASANT overlooking the harbor. The first Alhambra Hall (*c.* 1847) was built by the MOUNT PLEASANT FERRY COMPANY. The present building was erected in the 1930s. Alhambra Park has been used as a town gathering place and picnic area since the early 1800s. The site is near SHELL HALL, the summer home of the PINCKNEY family of SNEE FARM. It is possible that the name "Alhambra" was given by Charles Pinckney, who, as U.S. ambassador to Spain in 1801, became enamored with the 13th-century Moorish castle of the same name located outside Granada, Spain.

ALLIGATOR – "There is in the mouth of their rivers, or in lakes near the sea," wrote Thomas Ashe in 1682, "a Creature . . . called the Alligator . . . whose scaly back is impenetrable, refusing a musket bullet to pierce it . . . a voracious greedy creature, devouring whatever it seizes on . . . " From the Spanish *el lagarto*, meaning "lizard," the American alligator can reach a length of 19 feet. The alligator's primary food is fish, yet they are known for their indiscriminate diet and any animal within reach of their powerful jaws is fair game, especially dogs.

ALLYON de, LUCAS VASQUEZ – 16th-century Spanish explorer (also known as Vasquez) who established the first settlement on the Carolina coast in 1526. Thought to be located near present-day Georgetown, the small settlement was called SAN MIGUEL DE GUALDAPE and failed after six months. (see CHICORA)

ANDERSON, MAJOR ROBERT (1805–1871) – Union commander of FORT MOULTRIE and FORT SUMTER at the outset of the CIVIL WAR. Anderson's father, Richard C. Anderson, had served at Fort Moultrie during the REVOLUTIONARY WAR. Anderson was a West Point man and a firm Unionist, yet as a slave owner from Kentucky, he held conflicting sentiments concerning state's rights. After his command at Sumter, Anderson was posted in Washington, where he retired as a brigadier general in 1863 due to ill health. After the fall of the Confederacy in 1865, Anderson returned to Fort Sumter in a ceremony to raise the American flag over the fort (the same flag he had personally lowered four years earlier). President Lincoln was to have been at this ceremony, but chose instead to stay in Washington, where, that evening, he attended a play at Ford's Theater. (see BEAUREGARD, DOUBLEDAY, FORT SUMTER)

ANDERSONVILLE – This plantation was just north of THE GROVE overlooking SEWEE Bay on the mainland seacoast. Here also was a small enclave of summer cottages for neighboring plantation owners. The Anderson family was in CAROLINA at least by 1756, when David Anderson married Marie Jourdan in ST. THOMAS PARISH. In 1760, Joseph Anderson married Elizabeth Fitch in the house of James Anderson in ST. JAMES SANTEE. Daniel Anderson married Mary Esther Dubois in 1794. Captain James Anderson married Mary HAMLIN, daughter of Thomas Hamlin, in 1820. Their son, 2nd Lieutenant James Anderson (1828–1864), was killed during the CIVIL WAR fighting with the ST. JAMES MOUNTED RIFLEMEN. Members of the Anderson family are buried at OLD WAPPETAW cemetery. The plantation was later a landholding of William A. King, a mayor of MOUNT PLEASANT. (see CIVIL WAR)

ANDERSONVILLE CUT – This narrow creek near ANDERSONVILLE winds its way through the marsh from the INTRACOASTAL WATERWAY to BULL'S BAY. GENERAL SHERMAN sent Federal forces under Brigadier General E.E. Potter here in February 1865 with orders to march on Charleston from the east. This area was the site of the final engagement between Confederate and Union forces prior to the Federal occupation of Charleston. (see CIVIL WAR)

ANISECAU – Variation of ONESICAU, the SEWEE name for BULL'S ISLAND. In 1696, Samuel Hartley received a warrant for the island "commonly called Anisecau." In 1680, Hartley sold to Thomas Cary 1,580 acres on the island "known by ye name of One-si-cau." (see BULL'S ISLAND, SEWEE)

ARABIAN, U.S.S. – On January 2, 1848, the brigantine *Arabian* left FORT MOULTRIE with 100 additional recruits from South Carolina's Palmetto Regiment for Vera Cruz, part of 275 reinforcements sent to join the fight in

Mexico. Only two days later, the *Courier* reported the arrival of the schooner *Susan Safford* with the remains of those in the Palmetto Regiment who had been killed in the Mexican War. South Carolina gave full support to the war with Mexico, and most of the troops were mustered at Fort Moultrie. "The Palmettos," under Colonel Pierce M. Butler, was originally mustered at just less than 1,000 men; 422 died in Mexico, with 79 later dying of wounds or exposure.

ARBUTHNOT, FORT – Briefly, the name given by the British to FORT MOULTRIE following their occupation of Charleston in 1780. The name honored Admiral Mariot Arbuthnot, R.N., who commanded the fleet that supported the British takeover of Charleston. (see REVOLUTIONARY WAR)

ASHLEY RIVER – The Indians called the river running on the south side of the Charleston peninsula KIAWAH. It was renamed by the English to honor Lord ANTHONY ASHLEY COOPER. This relatively short tidal river has its headwaters in Wassamassaw Swamp about 40 miles above Charleston. The original colonial settlement was on the Ashley River at ALBEMARLE POINT (now Charles Towne Landing). Plantations on both sides of the river were given primarily to the cultivation of RICE. While most were working plantations, some were built as showplaces, such as Middleton Gardens, Magnolia-on-the-Ashley, and Drayton Hall, all now open to the public. The majority of the Ashley River plantation houses were destroyed by Federal troops in 1865. (see CIVIL WAR, POTTER'S RAIDERS)

ATLANTIC BEACH HOTEL – A grand hotel on SULLIVAN'S ISLAND in the late 1800s.

ATLANTICVILLE – Name of the center section of SULLIVAN'S ISLAND (near Station 22) first developed in the late 1800s. The NEW BRIGHTON HOTEL was the centerpiece of Atlanticville's Ocean Park. It was destroyed by fire and later replaced by the ATLANTIC BEACH HOTEL. Both were grand beachfront hotels, known for elegant lodging, fine dining, music, and weekend "hops" or dances. A large pavilion faced the front beach, with a boardwalk and bathhouses jutting into the surf. There were also private homes and cottages in Atlanticville. The July 3, 1885 *Courier* noted that "Captain Conner has one of the neatest and prettiest gardens on the island. The house is next west of the New Brighton Hotel." The area is now Sullivan's Island's "business" district. (see NEW BRIGHTON HOTEL)

AUDUBON, JOHN JAMES (1785–1851) – This noted artist and naturalist was a frequent visitor to Charleston and the EAST COOPER area in the early 1800s, where he collected many bird and animal skins for research and paintings. Several paintings in his *Birds of America* portfolio were drawn from the MOUNT PLEASANT shoreline. Audubon had many friends in Charleston, including Dr.

JOHN BACHMAN and CAPTAIN N.L. COSTE. In 1832, an entire barrel of bird skins packed in rum aboard the *Nimrod*, of which Captain Coste was master, went overboard in a sudden gale. Coste was able to save another barrel containing herons, cormorants, and two red-headed vultures. Both Coste and Bachman shared Audubon's interest in science and nature. Bachman and Audubon co-authored *The Quadrupeds of America*. Coste was the captain for Audubon's expeditions in Florida and the Gulf of Mexico. In 1907, the Audubon Society was organized in South Carolina for the protection of fish, birds, and game. (see DR. JOHN BACHMAN, CAPTAIN N.L. COSTE, RAVENEL)

AWENDAW – Also variously spelled as *Oiendaw*, *Owendaw*, *Awindaw*, and *Atwin-da-boo*. This rural community approximately 20 miles north of MOUNT PLEASANT is named for a SEWEE village, possibly the same place the first English colonists visited in April 1670 after landing at BULL'S ISLAND. Explorer and surveyor JOHN LAWSON stopped here in 1701, calling the place *Avendaugh-bough*, a variant spelling of *Awendaw-boo*. The Native American addition of "-boo" to a place name usually indicated a creek or watercourse. Awendaw Creek is also noted as SEEWEE RIVER on early maps. This area was part of the original SEWEE BARONY and a MANIGAULT plantation holding until the late 1800s. Other early-18th-century landowners included Joseph Wigfall, John Collins of TIBWIN, and John Barksdale. (see CONCISE HISTORY, SEWEE BARONY, SEWEE INDIANS)

BACHMAN, DR. JOHN (1790–1874) – For more than 50 years, Bachman was the pastor of Charleston's oldest Lutheran Church, St. John's. An avid naturalist, the Bachman warbler and Bachman sparrow were named for him. Bachman was a close friend to AUDUBON, and the two co-authored *The Quadrupeds of America*. Their friendship also resulted in familial ties, with Audubon's sons marrying Bachman's daughters. The Bachman family was one of the earliest to summer on SULLIVAN'S ISLAND.

BAHAI DE CAYAGUA – Name given to Charleston harbor by 16th-century Spanish explorers, *Cayagua* being the Spanish corruption of *KIAWAH*.

BALD EAGLE – "Of great strength and spirit," wrote naturalist Mark CATESBY of the American bald eagle (*Haliaetus leucocephaltis*). These majestic birds have a wingspan of over 6 feet and have made a strong comeback in coastal South Carolina. Their nests are huge, elaborate affairs built in the tops of dead trees or power poles, often used year after year by the same nesting pair, who mate for life. Their primary diet is fish, although they also prey on smaller birds and mammals. (see OSPREY)

BANDSTAND – The bandstand at the park on SULLIVAN'S ISLAND in front of the "hill fort" on Middle Street at Station 20 was originally built in 1904 as the

FORT MOULTRIE bandstand. When the fort was decommissioned in 1947, the bandstand was converted into a private residence on the south end of the island. In 1989, it was moved to its present location and rebuilt, once again, as the town bandstand. (see BATTERIES & FORTIFICATIONS)

BARBADOS – This 66-square-mile island in the West Indies was settled by the British in 1627 and, by the mid-1600s, considered one of the most densely populated areas in the world. Barbadian planters, particularly Sir John COLLETON, thus looked to the unsettled province of CAROLINA as a means for future growth and prosperity. The Carolina colony became, by and large, an experimental extension of the English colonial effort in Barbados. Almost one-half of the Carolina colony was made up of people from Barbados in the first 20 years of settlement. Dr. Henry Woodward, George Dearsley, Robert Daniell, and John GODFREY were among those originally from Barbados—also pirate STEDE BONNET. Ultimately the Barbadian influence was the standard on which the Carolina colony's political, social, and political structure was based. (see CONCISE HISTORY; also CHURCH ACT)

BARKSDALE'S POINT – The 17th-century name given to the easternmost point of old MOUNT PLEASANT (near the OLD BRIDGE) and named for John Barksdale (1657–1727), who owned the property in 1696. Barksdale had numerous landholdings, including a tract of land near AWENDAW. The Barksdale family retained ownership of much of this area until 1727. Barksdale's granddaughter, Elizabeth (d. 1781), was married to Andrew HIBBEN. The Indians called this area OLDWANUS POINT, meaning unknown. It is also seen on early maps as Old Woman's Point and NORTH POINT.

BARONY – Under the FUNDAMENTAL CONSTITUTIONS OF CAROLINA, there were two classes of nobility in Carolina: landgraves and CASSIQUES. Each landgrave received a barony of 48,000 acres; each cassique, 24,000 acres. Almost all of lowcountry South Carolina was originally segmented into baronies, although, for reasons unknown, no barony was granted to the East Cooper area proper. SEWEE BARONY was near AWENDAW. Similarly, on the Cooper River's EAST BRANCH were CYPRESS BARONY and QUINBY BARONY. WADBOO and WISKINBOO Barony formed the lower part of ST. JOHN'S PARISH, BERKELEY. (see COLLETON, MANIGAULT, WEST BRANCH)

BARRIER ISLAND – Usually thin and elongated, the barrier islands that line the South Carolina coast form a barrier, or line of defense, which protects the mainland against storms and the sea. Fronted by a beach of hard-packed sand and several rows of sand dunes, the barrier island is one of nature's most adaptive entities—a dynamic, ever-changing place that is constantly reshaping itself, accreting or eroding with the variables of wind and weather. While erosion causes problems with man's habitation of these islands, it is this continuous motion that allows the barrier island to survive. Depending upon an island's size, the interior can be thickly vegetated with pine, cedar, oak, MYRTLE, and PALMETTO. SULLIVAN'S ISLAND, ISLE OF PALMS, DEWEES, CAPERS, and BULL'S are all barrier islands. (see HUNTING ISLANDS)

BARTLAM POTTERY – In the 1760s, taking advantage of a vein of kaolin clay in the subsoil, Englishman John Bartlam established the first known American creamware pottery factory at a site on DANIEL ISLAND just below CAINHOY, naming his pottery "Queen's Ware." Bartlam had previously worked as a potter with Josiah Wedgwood in England. When Wedgwood traveled to America in 1765, he considered Bartlam a substantial threat, writing that Bartlam's Queen's Ware was "equal to any imported [into the colonies]." Bartlam's endeavor eventually failed and few examples of this rare American pottery remain.

BARTRAM – Philadelphia botanist John Bartram (1699–1777) kept up a regular correspondence with, and also visited friends in, CHARLES TOWN who shared his enthusiasm for botany, the continued discovery of new plants, and plant propagation. His alliance with the LOGAN and Hopton families brought him and, later, his son William (1739–1823) to their plantations on the upper WANDO RIVER. In 1763, William, referred to as "Billy," wrote in his journal, "set out with Mr. Hopton to his seat which he called starve gut hall on Wando River. He shewed me his rice ground & we walked in his Salt swamps." (see HOPTON, STARVEGUT HALL, LEXINGTON PLANTATION, WANDO PLANTATION)

BATTERY, THE – Popular name given to the promenade at White Point at the tip of peninsular Charleston. It was originally called White Point or Oyster Point for the spit of bleached oyster shells that showed at low tide. The location was always strategically important to the city, and batteries were periodically erected there for protection, including Fort Broughton in 1735 and Fort Wilkins in 1812. It was here that the pirate STEDE BONNET was hanged in 1717. Earthworks and guns lined the site during the CIVIL WAR. The promenade known as High Battery was built in 1838. (see BATTERIES & FORTIFICATIONS)

BEAUREGARD, GENERAL PIERRE G.T. (1818–1893) – Confederate hero and commander of Confederate forces in Charleston at the outset of the Civil War. He had been one of Major ROBERT ANDERSON'S artillery students at West Point. BATTERY BEAUREGARD on SULLIVAN'S ISLAND was named in his honor. (see ANDERSON, CIVIL WAR)

BEECHER, GENERAL JAMES CHAPLIN (1828–1886) – Congregationalist minister and the brother of abolitionist Harriet Beecher Stowe, Beecher was in Charleston as part of the Union occupation in 1865. He and his wife resided in MOUNT PLEASANT for a time, and it is said that she, personally, held the torch to burn the house at LAUREL HILL Plantation. At nearby OAKLAND

PLANTATION, she was prevented from doing so only at the urging of the former slaves. DR. JOHN IRVING in *A Day on the Cooper River* tells of General Beecher's visit to LIMERICK Plantation in 1865. Served wine with dinner and fearing that it might have been poisoned, he first called one of his soldiers over to serve as a taster. When the soldier refused, Beecher called for one of the house servants to taste the wine. Finally, the owner of the plantation, William J. Ball, took the first sip "to show what he thought of him." Afterwards, the house and barns were ransacked and the lawn littered with papers, including a rare elephant edition of AUDUBON'S *Birds of America*. Beecher took his own life in 1886. (see CIVIL WAR, POTTER'S RAIDERS)

BEEHIVE – A community off Highway 17 North just above WHITEHALL Plantation and overlooking COPAHEE SOUND, it takes its name from the Bee family plantation located there in the 19th century. This is one of the many settlements evolving from lands given to newly freed slaves following the Civil War. (see SLAVERY)

BELVUE-BERMUDA PLANTATION – On the Wando River at LONG POINT on the north side of HOBCAW Creek. This plantation was owned by Nicholas VENNING Jr. in the early 1800s. More than likely, the early settlement of BERMUDA TOWN was located on or near this plantation. (see VENNING)

BERESFORD, RICHARD (d. 1722) – Originally from BARBADOS, Richard Beresford had acquired almost 5,000 acres by 1711 in ST. THOMAS and CHRIST CHURCH Parishes. Beresford's public career was equally impressive. He served on the Grand Council, in the assembly, as commissioner of the Indian trade, and was public treasurer, a position he held throughout the proprietary period. In 1708, he was made the Lords Proprietors deputy for CAROLINA. His DANIEL ISLAND holdings included his home plantation, BERESFORD HALL. He provided monies for building the first parish church of ST. THOMAS in 1707. He died in March 17, 1722, killed "by a falling tree limb." Of his sizable estate, he left one-third to establish a free school, which became known as the BERESFORD BOUNTY, monies for education of the poor that have remained in use for over 300 years. This trust now goes toward the upkeep of ST. THOMAS CHURCH. His son was Richard Beresford Jr. (1720–1772).

BERESFORD BOUNTY – The name of the trust established by Richard BERESFORD (above). BERESFORD also was the name given to the plantation lands near CAINHOY where a free school was established with this trust. From the March 3, 1765 *Gazette*: "TO BE LETT, or SOLD, That plantation in St. Thomas's Parish, adjoining Bereford's Bounty (or more properly the Free-School) known by the name of SAW-PIT, containing about 520 acres, only one mile distant from the parish-church, not so far from Cainhoy meeting, and 16 miles from Charles-Town: It has on it a good shade for making bricks, very good clay, and plenty of wood to burn them for several years, and a good landing on a navigable creek, just above the cut in Cooper-River."

BERESFORD CREEK – A deepwater creek which forms the north, east, and western boundaries of DANIEL ISLAND, named for colonist and early Daniel Island landowner RICHARD BERESFORD. The western branch of the creek flowing into the COOPER RIVER was originally called ITTCHICAW. The eastern side flowing into the WANDO RIVER was called WATCOW, variously spelled as WATROO and WATTICOE, undoubtedly names given by the ETIWAN Indians who originally lived on the island.

BERESFORD HALL – Name of RICHARD BERESFORD's plantation on BERESFORD CREEK. It was established *c.* 1706 on a bluff overlooking BERESFORD CREEK. When it was put up for sale in 1760 by Richard Beresford Jr., it was described as being "950 acres, upon a creek leading from Wando to Coosaw [Cooper] River, 12 miles from town." The plantation was then purchased by Charleston furniture-maker Thomas Elfe. This plantation grew market crops and also had a working brickyard on the creek. (see BRICKMAKING)

BERKELEY COUNTY – From 1883 to 1889, the town of MOUNT PLEASANT was the county seat of Berkeley County. The name honored LORDS PROPRIETORS William and John Berkeley. The county courthouse building on PITT STREET is now known as the DARBY BUILDING.

BERMUDA TOWN – Laid out prior to 1699, this 45-acre settlement was located on LONG POINT on the WANDO RIVER. Few records remain to tell of this community; it may have been a planned town that never saw full habitation. It is first mentioned in 1699 when James Allen Jr. deeds to Thomas Fry, "25 acres or thereabouts Northward upon the Broad Path or Common High Road that leads from Sewee to Bermuda Town." In 1716, George LOGAN was requested to measure the land "belonging to the schoolhouse at Bermuda Town" for the use of CHRIST CHURCH. A 1726 deed refers to "70 acres situate on a part of Hobcaw Neck commonly called Bermudoes Town." In 1734, 50 acres were deeded to Joseph Wragg "in Bermuda Town." The town, if it existed, disappears after this. The name, however, continued on with the later VENNING landholding BELVUE-BERMUDA PLANTATION. The name perhaps had an original association with colonists arriving from the island of Bermuda.

BIDDY – A common word for a baby chicken, from the African word *bidi-bidi*, meaning "bird." (see GULLAH)

BIGGIN – Area on the upper COOPER RIVER's east bank (also spelled variously as *Biggon*). The place may have taken its name from Biggin Hill in Kent, England, or it may have been drawn from a Native American word. The church was located on

TIPPYCUTLAW Hill on the land given by Landgrave John COLLETON specifically for the erection of a parish church for lower ST. JOHN'S PARISH, BERKELEY. The first church, built *c.* 1712, burned in 1755. The second church served until 1781, when, during the REVOLUTIONARY WAR, it was a garrison and storehouse for British soldiers. It was set afire upon their departure. Rebuilt again, the third church was burned in a forest fire in the 1890s and was never rebuilt. Only the brick walls remain today. (see STRAWBERRY CHAPEL, STRAWBERRY FERRY)

BIGGIN'S BRIDGE, BATTLE OF – On April 12, 1780, British General Sir Banestre Tarleton surprised and defeated American troops under Colonel William Washington and General Isaac HUGER, killing 30 American dragoons and capturing 60 more. This was one of a series of skirmishes that occurred in the EAST BRANCH and WEST BRANCH areas in 1780–81. (see BATTLE OF HOG ISLAND CHANNEL, HUGER, MARION, REVOLUTIONARY WAR, VIDEAU BRIDGE, WADBOO)

BLACK DRINK – The ceremonial tea used by Native Americans in rituals and as a cleansing purge. It was made from the toasted leaves of the CASSINA bush, also known as YAUPON. (see CASSINA)

BLACK SKIMMER – These streamlined black-and-white sea birds (*Rynchops niger*) were called the "Cut Water" by naturalist MARK CATESBY for the way they glide low over marsh creeks, skimming the top of the water with their lower bill in search of food. When the bill hits a shrimp or small fish, it snaps shut. They are also colloquially known as "shear waters."

BLACKBEARD – Alias for the nefarious pirate, William Teach (or Thatch). In May 1718, Blackbeard (with 5 ships and 400 men) sailed into Charleston harbor, seized the pilot boat and a number of other vessels, and took hostages, including Samuel Wragg, a prominent merchant and member of the Provincial Congress. Blackbeard threatened to kill the hostages unless he was provided with certain medicines. The demand was met and the hostages were freed. Blackbeard sailed off, to be captured shortly afterward off the North Carolina coast in a bloody sea battle with Robert Maynard. It took five thrusts of a sword and repeated pistol shots to kill him. Maynard then sailed into Bath, North Carolina, with Blackbeard's head on the bowsprit. (see STEDE BONNET, PIRATES)

BLESSING, THE – This former RICE plantation on the east shore of the Cooper River's EAST BRANCH was first granted to colonist Jonah LYNCH in 1682, at a "place called Wattesaw also the Blessing." WATTESAW was the Native American word for the area, meaning unknown. It was at times a Bonneau, Deas, and POYAS landholding. In the late 1700s, it was owned by John Laurens. An advertisement for the sale of the plantation in the 1840s describes it as containing "1,000 acres of Land, best part thereof being extraordinary Corn and Rice Land, very will timbered, and good Cedar posts in the Swamp." It is presumed that the name "Blessing" came from the ship of the same name that brought Jonah Lynch to the colonies in 1671.

BLOCKADE RUNNING – The name given to the extensive import-export trade conducted during the Federal blockade of Southern ports during the CIVIL WAR. Charleston was a major blockade running port, and during the four years of the war, some 250 ships ran or attempted to run through the blockading fleet offshore. All manner of vessels were refitted to become blockade runners, many converted or built at HOBCAW Shipyard. Covered by the guns of FORT MOULTRIE, blockade runners took the SWASH CHANNEL, hugging the SULLIVAN'S ISLAND shoreline. This route was dangerous because of the rocks at the GRILLAGE and several ships sank or ran aground in the attempt. Despite its dangers, blockade running was vital in order for the Confederacy to receive goods from abroad and export RICE and COTTON from the Southern states. (see BREACH INLET, CAPE ROMAIN, *CELT*, CIVIL WAR, *COFFEE*, HIBBEN, *HOUSATONIC*, *HUNLEY*, JONES SHIPYARD, *PLANTER*, *PRESTO*, SWASH CHANNEL)

BLUE CRAB – A ten-legged crustacean, the Atlantic blue crab (*Callinectes sapidus*) is so named for the striking blue coloration on its claws. Male blue crabs are locally known as JIMMIES; females, as SHE-CRABS.

BONEYARD – The northeast beachfront area of BULL'S ISLAND. The name was given for the massive driftwood forest lining the beach, the sun-bleached tree limbs resembling dinosaur bones.

BONNEAU BEACH – Located near PORCHER's bluff on the seacoast of mainland MOUNT PLEASANT, the marshland flats here overlooking COPAHEE SOUND were used in the mid-19th century for the Bonneau and Leland Salt Works. An advertisement in February 1865 offering the salt works for sale noted that the business had the capacity of making 30 to 40 bushels of salt per day. Dr. Peter Porcher Bonneau (1816–1871) of nearby LAUREL HILL Plantation was a signer of the Ordinance of Secession for CHRIST CHURCH PARISH and later served as a surgeon with the 10th S.C. Cavalry. (see Bonneau, SEASIDE PLANTATION)

BONNEAU FERRY – On the Cooper River's EAST BRANCH just above FRENCH QUARTER CREEK, the ferry adjoining this 11,000-acre RICE plantation was an important crossing point between plantation lands on both sides of the river. The patriarch of the Bonneau family was Antoine Bonneau (*c.* 1645–1700) of Rochelle, France, who came to CAROLINA as a HUGUENOT émigré. In his will, he left his sons, Samuel and Benjamin, 3,020 acres of land "including the plantation where he lived at the Ferry in St. John's Parish." The Bonneau Ferry landing also served as a supply point for area plantations in the transporting of LUMBER and other goods to town by boat. In the early 1800s, the plantation was known as PRIOLI during its ownership by the Prioleau family.

BONNET, STEDE (d. 1718) – Called "The Gentleman Pirate," Bonnet had been a respectable citizen of BARBADOS with the rank of major before taking up pirating. In 1717, he allied with BLACKBEARD and began marauding ships off the Carolinas. Colonel WILLIAM RHETT was dispatched from Charleston in 1718 to go after Bonnet, eventually capturing him at Cape Fear. Brought back to Charleston, tried, and condemned to death for piracy, Bonnet escaped jail and, dressed as a woman, fled to SULLIVAN'S ISLAND, where he apparently had arranged to be picked up by the pirate Christopher Moody, whose ship was offshore. Bonnet hid on the island for ten days before he was caught. He was hanged at White Point (the BATTERY) on December 10, 1718, and buried ignominiously in the marsh below the low-water mark. (see PIRATES)

BONNEY, ANNE – Called "The Lady Pirate," she was the illegitimate daughter of an attorney from County Cork, Ireland, who had immigrated to CHARLES TOWN. A boisterous girl of "fierce and courageous temper," she became infatuated with the pirate Calico Jack Rackam and, disguised in sailor's clothes, went to sea with him, often dressing as a male pirate during raids on ships. The two were captured and convicted of piracy in Jamaica in 1720. As she was pregnant, Bonney was released. Calico Jack, however, was executed. Some believe she eventually returned to Charles Town and married, disappearing into respectable obscurity. (see PIRATES)

BOONE HALL PLANTATION – Located in MOUNT PLEASANT on Horlbeck Creek, the land for this plantation was originally granted to Major John Boone (1645–1711) in the late 1600s. Boone was 25 when he arrived in 1670 from BARBADOS. Like other early colonists, his goal was to acquire a large acreage on which he could plant a money crop suitable for the export trade. His "Boone Hall" eventually grew to a 17,000-acre plantation producing cotton and staple crops, and during its ownership in the 1800s by the Horlbeck family, it became one of the largest BRICKMAKING concerns in the region. The much-photographed avenue of over 80 live OAKS dates to 1743 and was planted by Captain Thomas Boone. The brick slave cabins date to the early 1800s. Boone Hall now comprises 738 acres and remains a working plantation that includes a grove of peach trees. The house museum and grounds are open to the public. It is on the National Register of Historic Places. (see BRICKMAKING, BRICKYARD PLANTATION)

BOOTLEGGING – During Prohibition, the remote woods, swamps, and inlets of the lowcountry were ideal for both the making and smuggling of illegal liquor. HELL HOLE SWAMP was famous for its bootlegging activities as well as parts of the SANTEE RIVER. (see MOONSHINE)

BOSSIS PLANTATION – Former RICE plantation on the western shore of the Cooper River's EAST BRANCH. Some say the name may come from an early landowner by the name of Bosse; others surmise the name came from plantation slaves who called it "the boss's" plantation. The original house, which burned in 1909, was built by John Harleston in 1736. Bossis is one of the few plantations that was inhabited following the CIVIL WAR, and Harleston family members continued to live there until the 1920s.

BOUNDARY STREET – Now SIMMONS STREET, this street running from COLEMAN BOULEVARD to CENTER STREET in MOUNT PLEASANT once marked the northeastern boundary of the OLD VILLAGE. It was renamed for Yonge Simmons, mayor of Mount Pleasant in 1916 and from 1921 to 1928.

BOWATT – Also variously spelled as *Bowat* and *Boowatt*, the name given for both the creek and the surrounding land area on the MOUNT PLEASANT seacoast mainland overlooking COPAHEE SOUND. The name is undoubtedly of Native American origin, their use of "-boo" or "-bou" being a designation for a watercourse. Colonist George Dearsley had perhaps the earliest holdings here, and records show that in 1696, he sold 1,300 acres "on Boowatt Creek" to Thomas Hamlin. In 1702, Captain William Capers had a warrant for "400 acres in Boowatt" on lands located "north of John Hamlin on Copahee." The Hamlin family continues to retain property in this area.

BOWMAN'S JETTY – The name given to the rocks in front of FORT MOULTRIE on the beach at SULLIVAN'S ISLAND, popularly referred to as the GRILLAGE. Designed and built in the 1830s and 1840s by Captain Alexander H. Bowman (d. 1865) of the U.S. Army Corps of Engineers, these rock groins were built upon a crib work, or grillage, of palmetto logs filled with sand and granite. Bowman graduated third in his class at West Point in 1825 and, for much of his career, was an instructor of mathematics and engineering there. His successful attempt at beachfront erosion management continues to protect the south end of the island from erosion. The easternmost groin was lengthened by 30 feet when the JETTIES were erected. (see BLOCKADE RUNNING, JETTIES)

BRABANT – This former RICE plantation near the FRENCH QUARTER in ST. THOMAS PARISH was once several different tracts originally deeded between 1704 and 1720 to various French HUGUENOT émigrés, including the Pagett, Potevin, Carteau, and Belin families. The largest of the tracts was deeded to Daniel Brabant in 1709, thus the plantation's name. During the REVOLUTIONARY WAR, it was the country seat of Bishop Robert Smith (who married Elizabeth Pagett) and it was here on January 3, 1782, at VIDEAU BRIDGE crossing FRENCH QUARTER CREEK, that Samuel VENNING killed British soldier "Mad Archie" Campbell. One of the plantation tracts, Pagett's Landing, also had a BRICKYARD. In the 1850s, the property was owned by Dr. EDMUND RAVENEL. (see THE GROVE)

BREACH INLET – The narrow inlet separating SULLIVAN'S ISLAND and ISLE OF PALMS, noted for its treacherous currents and deep holes. When explorer JOHN LAWSON attempted to cross "the Breach" in January 1701, there was not enough water at low tide to get a canoe across. By the REVOLUTIONARY WAR, the inlet was deep enough to prevent the British from fording across and attacking Fort Sullivan from the north. It was from Breach Inlet that the C.S.S. *HUNLEY* trained with practice dives and ultimately left to go after the U.S.S. *HOUSATONIC*. The first bridge across the inlet was erected in 1898 when ISLE OF PALMS resort was first established.

BRICKMAKING – Taking advantage of a rich vein of orange-red clay that lies just underneath the earth's surface, numerous BRICKYARDS were located on the WANDO and COOPER Rivers during the 18th and 19th centuries. This lucrative industry began in earnest after a series of disastrous fires in CHARLES TOWN and subsequent laws requiring all buildings to be erected of brick. Between 1745 and 1860, more than 50 brickyards came into operation in the EAST COOPER area, with more than 30 on the Wando River and its tributaries alone. (see ADDISON'S BRICKYARD, BERESFORD HALL, BERESFORD CREEK, BOONE HALL, BRABANT, BRICKYARD PLANTATION, CAINHOY, DANIEL ISLAND, ELM GROVE, FOGARTIE CREEK, LIME KILN, MORELAND, O'HEAR'S POINT, PALMETTO GROVE, PARKER ISLAND, TOOMER'S BRICKYARD, VILLEPONTOUX, WAMPANCHECOONE, WANDO RIVER)

BRICKYARD, THE – A plantation, also known as MORELAND on the COOPER RIVER just above CLEMENT'S FERRY. In 1819, Alfred HUGER sold the plantation to John Gordon, who established a brickyard and "thereby realized a great fortune." In 1842, it came into possession of Governor Thomas Bennett, who had married Gordon's widow. It was one of the largest BRICKMAKING concerns in the area. (see MORELAND)

BRICKYARD PLANTATION – Originally part of BOONE HALL Plantation, Brickyard was owned by the Horlbeck family in the 1800s. Master builders John and Peter Horlbeck came to CHARLES TOWN from Saxony in the mid-1700s. Under the ownership of their sons, John Jr. and Henry Horlbeck, Boone Hall's brickyard became one of the leading producers of brick in the Charleston area. An estimated 4 million bricks were made there in 1850. Boone Hall's brickyard was one of the few WANDO RIVER brickyards to continue operations following the CIVIL WAR. Extant ruins on Horlbeck Creek include the tall brick boiler chimney, brick commissary, and various outbuildings.

BRIDGE OF BOATS – In 1776, while Fort Sullivan was being hastily erected, there was no bridge linking SULLIVAN'S ISLAND and MOUNT PLEASANT. Crossing troops and supplies was of paramount importance. General CHARLES LEE, commander of the American forces, felt an escape route from the fort was vital since he viewed the unfinished fort as a "slaughter pen," precariously undermanned and inadequate. After various unsuccessful attempts at constructing some sort of sturdy crossing, a string of flatboats was anchored across COVE INLET in a line, becoming known as the "bridge of boats" or LEE'S BRIDGE. Remains of this bridge could still be seen in the 1850s. Its location was near the present ruins of the OLD BRIDGE. (see COVE INLET, LEE'S BRIDGE, REVOLUTIONARY WAR)

BUCKET FACTORY – Located on the south side of SHEM CREEK in the mid-1800s, the Mount Pleasant Bucket Factory was owned by John HAMLIN and provided painted and unpainted pine, cypress, an assortment of lumber, lathes, and, of course, buckets. An advertisement in the April 24, 1854 *Courier* corrected the misinformation that the Bucket Factory had closed, stating that operations ". . . had merely been suspended shortly for repairs." FACTORY STREET, now a part of Live Oak Drive, was named for this business.

BULL'S BAY – Large bay lying to the north of BULL'S ISLAND and extending to CAPE ROMAIN. The village of McCLELLANVILLE fronts the mainland. LIGHTHOUSE ISLAND is on its northern edge. It was here that the *Carolina* made anchorage with the original Charleston colonists in 1670. Bull's Bay has historically been dangerous for shipping. Shallow, it can become unstable with even a sudden squall, and numerous vessels have been grounded or sunk here throughout history. (see ANDERSONVILLE CUT, BLOCKADE RUNNING, CIVIL WAR, CONCISE HISTORY)

BULL'S ISLAND – The northernmost and largest of the string of BARRIER ISLANDS stretching from Charleston Harbor to CAPE ROMAIN. It was on the north end of Bull's Island that the original English settlers first made landfall in April 1670. This was one of the HUNTING ISLANDS of the SEWEE Indians, who called the island ONESICAU. The island was later named for Stephen Bull, who had a grant for the island in 1696. For a time, it was owned by John Collins of TIBWIN. When JOHN LAWSON stopped here in January 1701, he wrote that there were "a great many Cattel and Hogs upon it; the Cattel being very wild, and the Hogs very lean." He also added, "we found such Swarms of Musquitoes, and other troblesome Insects, that we got but little Rest that Night." A COASTAL WATCH was erected on the island in 1707, manned by "one white man and two Sewee Indians," and the TABBY ruins of an octagonal fort on the back side of the island may be the remains of this early outpost. Now uninhabited, the island is the centerpiece of the CAPE ROMAIN National Wildlife Refuge. It has proved a successful site for the introduction of the red wolf into the coastal Carolina habitat. (see CONCISE HISTORY)

BUTT, U.S.S. *ARCHIE* – The cement hull seen in the marsh at PATRIOT'S POINT just to the right of the COOPER RIVER BRIDGE is all that remains of a supply ship that served FORT MOULTRIE at the turn of the 20th century. The vessel was named after Major Archibald Butt, advisor to Presidents Theodore Roosevelt and William Howard Taft. Born in 1866 in Augusta, Georgia, Butt graduated in 1888 from the University of the South, Sewanee. While in Washington, where he served as Secretary to the Mexican Embassy, he developed strong friendships with both Roosevelt and Taft and served as a military advisor to both. A first-class passenger on the *Titanic* when it sank in 1908, Butt was lauded by survivors for his heroism in helping the women and children into the lifeboats.

CAINHOY – The earliest record of Cainhoy as a place name is found in Joel Gascoyne's "Map of the Country of Carolina," drawn in 1682. The distinctive bend at the upper WANDO RIVER is marked with the name, "Kenha." Undoubtedly, the name is of Native American origin, the meaning long since lost. Early colonists included a large number of Congregationalist DISSENTERS, and by 1698, the first church, the CAINHOY MEETING HOUSE, had been erected. A sizable village grew up at Cainhoy, the location particularly important since it was here that the CAINHOY FERRY connected those in ST. THOMAS PARISH with those in CHRIST CHURCH PARISH. By the 19th century, Cainhoy was the commercial hub for the surrounding area plantations, particularly those inland tracts without direct river access. The How Tavern was here in the mid-1700s. It was here, also, that the parsonage for ST. THOMAS CHURCH was built, wherein the BERESFORD BOUNTY free school was held for much of the 19th century.

CAINHOY FERRY – The ferry crossing the WANDO RIVER from the village of CAINHOY into CHRIST CHURCH PARISH was important to transportation in this region in the 18th and 19th centuries. The ferry was at different periods under the care of various persons who had landholdings at Cainhoy. In 1744, it was vested to Robert How, who also established a school at Cainhoy. By the 1760s, the ferry was under the care of Joseph FOGARTIE, who also brokered the transportation of various goods through his concern, Fogartie's Landing. In 1846, it was vested to Ferdinand GREGORIE of WANDO PLANTATION. In 1853, it was invested to John O'Hear of O'HEAR'S POINT. Despite stories to the contrary, there never was a ferryman named Cain. The name "Cainhoy" was a derivative of "Kenha," an Indian name. (see GREGORIE)

CAINHOY MEETING HOUSE – Thought to be erected by 1698, when the first minister, Reverend Hugh Adams, served both this congregation and the one at WAPPETAW, this was a DISSENTERS meeting house, at first Congregationalist but, by 1723, referred to as the "Presbyterian Congregation at Cainehoi." The building no longer exists. The graveyard, however, retains gravestones of many early parishioners. Pastors at Cainhoy included the Reverend Josiah Smith, grandson of Governor Thomas Smith (1648–1694). His father, Dr. George Smith, was also a pastor at Cainhoy in 1728. It served as a hospital for American troops during the REVOLUTIONARY WAR; General William MOULTRIE wrote, "we have established a hospital at Cainhoy meeting-house, for all those who are not able to do duty, to repair to."

CALAIS & DOVER FERRY – The popular name given to SCOTT'S FERRY (later CLEMENT'S FERRY) on DANIEL ISLAND near CLOUTER CREEK. The name "Calais" arose because of the large number of French HUGUENOTS living on the eastern side of the COOPER RIVER. The landing on the western side of the river was dubbed "Dover" since the majority of landowners there were English or from BARBADOS. The name was a joking adaptation to the ferry that connects England and France. (see LESESNE)

CANDLEBERRY TREE – Early name for the Wax MYRTLE, also known as bayberry. Candles were usually made from either tallow or beeswax, but the berries of the wax myrtle also made a fragrant and slow burning candle. The berries were harvested in the fall and placed in a kettle of boiling water. As the wax rose to the top, it was skimmed off and strained. This process was repeated again and again until a cake of bayberry wax was eventually formed, then melted and poured into candle forms. Bayberry candles were considered better than those made of tallow and esteemed for their sweet aroma. (see MYRTLE)

CAPE ROMAIN – Jutting into the Atlantic just north of BULL'S BAY, the name *Capo Romano* was given to this distinctive coastal feature by Spanish explorers in the early 1500s. It is also found on later maps as Cape Carteret. A major physical feature of the eastern seaboard, it has historically been a significant area for shipping. PIRATES used the inlets and bays here as a hide-away. Both British and American naval vessels used its waters during the REVOLUTIONARY WAR, and it was an entry spot for Confederate BLOCKADE RUNNERS during the CIVIL WAR. A lighthouse has been on RACCOON KEY (also known as LIGHTHOUSE ISLAND) since 1847. A later lighthouse, built in 1858, is no longer in operation but stands as a day mark. The Cape Romain National Wildlife Refuge, established in 1930, contains 16 miles of pristine marshland, creeks, and waterways.

CAPERS ISLAND – This 3.5-mile BARRIER ISLAND just south of BULL'S ISLAND was named for William Capers, who settled in CAROLINA in 1684 and gained ownership of the island in 1702. The SEWEE Indians called the island HAWAN. Surveyor JOHN LAWSON stopped here in January 1701, calling it Dix's Island, writing that " . . . an honest Scot . . . gave the best Reception his Dwelling afforded, being well provided of Oat-Meal." Settled as plantation land until the 20th century, Capers Island is now an uninhabited wildlife refuge owned by the State of South Carolina. It is accessible only by boat. (see HUNTING ISLANDS)

CARNE, DR. SAMUEL – One of the first medical doctors in CHRIST CHURCH PARISH, Carne came to CAROLINA in 1740 and, in 1759, married Catherine Bond, daughter of Jacob Bond of HOBCAW Plantation. He established an apothecary in Charles Town with both Dr. Robert Wilson and Elisha Poinsett. In 1759, he was the port physician and a member of the assembly. His house on Tradd Street was called "The Orange Garden," and an advertisement in the October 11, 1760 *Gazette* states that Dr. Carne wished to sell " . . . orange trees in all sizes, which will be disposed of cheap, as he wants to clear part of his garden." Carne was a Loyalist and returned to England during the Revolution; his lands were confiscated following the war. (see ORANGES)

CAROLINA – In 1629, Charles I of England granted a proprietary charter to Sir Robert Heath, described as the area lying south of Virginia all the way across the continent, from ocean to ocean. This became known as *Carolana*, from the Latin *Carolanus*, meaning "Charles." After the restoration of Charles II of England, the Heath Charter was declared null and void and Carolina was given to eight LORDS PROPRIETORS.

CAROLINA – The flagship and largest of the fleet of three vessels to bring the original English colonists to Carolina in 1670. A frigate of about 100 feet and 200 tons, the ship carried a crew of 19 and accommodated 93 passengers. She is the only one of the three ships that made the voyage unharmed, finally making landfall at BULL'S ISLAND in March 1670. The captain of the *Carolina* was Henry Brayne. (see CONCISE HISTORY, also *ALBEMARLE*,)

CAROLINA BAYS – Unexplained, round geological depressions in the earth found along the Carolina coastal plain. Various theories postulate how the bays may have been formed. Some believe they were the result of impacts from ancient meteorites or perhaps a geological remnant of the last ice age. Often dense and swampy, the bays are repositories of a remarkably lush and abundant plant life. (see NAKED LADY LILY)

CAROLINA PACKET – Ship launched in 1771 at Captain Clement Lemprier's HOBCAW Shipyard. The *Carolina Packet* made regular runs between CHARLES TOWN and London.

CAROLINA PARAQUET (PARAKEET) – Beautifully painted by AUDUBON in his *Birds of America* portfolio, these brightly colored birds were once found in great abundance in coastal Carolina. They were forced into extinction when they were hunted for their plumage.

CASSINA – The cassina (*Ilex vomitoria*) is a small woody shrub indigenous to the coast, a member of the holly family, and also called YAUPON. The Indians made a beverage called the BLACK DRINK from the toasted leaves of cassina. In daily life, they used it much as we drink coffee today. For ceremonial use, they drank it in excess as a ritualistic purge. So popular was the Black Drink that cassina was a major article of trade between the coastal tribes and those inland. Taken moderately, the leaves of the cassina are a suitable substitute for tea, and during the 1930s and 1940s, several plantations along RIFLE RANGE ROAD grew cassina for this use. Cassina tea, however, never reached the hoped-for commercial success. Because of the bright red berries it produces during the winter, it was also known as the Christmas-berry Bush.

CASSIQUE – Also spelled *cacique*, the term given to an Indian king or chief. Also a class of nobility in Carolina during the proprietary period. (see BARONY, CONCISE HISTORY)

CASTLE PINCKNEY – Located in Charleston Harbor on the island named SHUTE'S FOLLY, the first fortification there was a horseshoe battery erected in 1742. The second, a wooden structure made of palisades and sand, was named to honor REVOLUTIONARY WAR patriot General Charles Cotesworth PINCKNEY (1746–1825). Destroyed by the hurricane of 1804, Castle Pinckney was rebuilt of brick and, by the War of 1812, was considered the most important fortification in Charleston harbor. The fort saw no action until the CIVIL WAR, when it was used as a holding place for Federal prisoners taken at the first Battle of Manassas (Bull Run). The island was later used as a light station and supply depot from 1878 to 1917. (see CIVIL WAR, PINCKNEY)

CAT ISLAND – Located in the upper reaches of the WANDO RIVER. In August 1760, Richard Beresford Jr. announced the sale of his plantation at Cat Island containing " . . . 125 acres, and the marshes about it, 777 acres, about 15 miles from town on Wando River."

CATESBY, MARK (*c.* 1679–1749) – A naturalist and artist, Catesby was one of the first to fully describe the flora and fauna of the Carolinas. His book, *The Natural History of Carolina, Florida and the Bahama Islands, with Observations on the Soil, Air and Water*, was first published in 1731. Catesby visited Charleston and explored the surrounding areas in 1710 and 1722. His descriptions of the Carolina Indian tribes, their customs, language, religions, and appearance are among the most complete written of that time. (see BALD EAGLE, CANDLEBERRY TREE, CONCISE HISTORY, MOCKINGBIRD, MYRTLE, JOHN LAWSON)

CEDAR – These tall, slender evergreens (*Juniperus silicicola*) grow profusely near marshes and on the BARRIER ISLANDS and produce clusters of small bluish berries similar to those of the wax MYRTLE tree. In colonial times, these berries were used for both medicinal purposes and as a home brew. Wrote explorer JOHN LAWSON in the early 1700s, "The Cedar Berries are infused, and made Beer of, by the Bermudians; they are Carminative and much of the Quality of Juniper-Berries."

C.S.S. *CELT* – BLOCKADE RUNNER that sank at the GRILLAGE in February 1865 attempting to leave Charleston harbor prior to the fall of the city to the Federal troops. (see BLOCKADE RUNNING, BOWMAN'S JETTY)

CENTER STREET – Running the eastern border of old MOUNT PLEASANT from the harbor to Ben Sawyer Boulevard, this street originally ran through the center of HILLIARDSVILLE, hence its name.

CHAINEY BRIAR – A wild asparagus that grows in vacant lots, ditches, and around the old forts on SULLIVAN'S ISLAND. The name is likely a GULLAH creation. This slender asparagus most likely adapted to the natural environment from seeds blown from the cultivated asparagus grown on area plantations.

CHALMERS, DR. LIONEL (1715–1777) – One of the first medical doctors in CHRIST CHURCH PARISH, *c.* 1750. Through his marriage to Martha LOGAN, he became an owner of WANDO PLANTATION. Dr. Chalmers set up a thriving practice in CHARLES TOWN and was the first to establish a weather station and furnish forecasts for the city. He was also one of the earliest to explore the connections between climate conditions and disease. His publications, printed in Charles Town and London, were among the most important to general medicine of that period. Chalmers Street in Charleston is named for him.

CHAPEL OF EASE – The name given to smaller churches in the various parishes created by the CHURCH ACT of 1706. These chapels were erected to be accessible to those plantations remote from the central parish church. They included POMPION HILL and STRAWBERRY CHAPEL. The small Episcopal church of St. James in McCLELLANVILLE and St. Andrew's in MOUNT PLEASANT also began as chapels of ease.

CHARLES TOWN – Name formally given to the settlement in 1679, in honor of the British monarch, Charles II. The name was abbreviated to "Charleston" in 1783, when the capital was moved to Columbia.

CHARLESTON & SEASHORE RAILROAD COMPANY – Name of the ferry and trolley system, *c.* 1900, that brought visitors from Charleston by ferry to MOUNT PLEASANT, where they then took the trolley over to SULLIVAN'S ISLAND and ISLE OF PALMS. (see *COMMODORE PERRY,* STATIONS)

CHENEY'S BOARDING HOUSE – Mrs. Cheney's Boarding House also known as THE PLANTER'S HOTEL was a popular summer retreat on SULLIVAN'S ISLAND at MOULTRIEVILLE, *c.* 1848.

CHEROKEE and *TAMAR* – Two British men-of-war in Charleston during the REVOLUTIONARY WAR. In 1776, within firing range of SULLIVAN'S

ISLAND, these ships initially hindered the construction of Fort Sullivan. To drive them off, WILLIAM MOULTRIE and a band of "gentlemen volunteers" left Charles Town under cover of a "dark and very cold night" and rowed across the harbor where, working all night, they erected a small battery at HADDRELL'S POINT, surprising the two ships the next morning with a cannonade from the newly built fortification. The ships were forced out of firing range, and work on Fort Sullivan was able to begin. They were also engaged by the *Defense* in the BATTLE OF HOG ISLAND CHANNEL. (see REVOLUTIONARY WAR)

CHICORA – An Indian tribe and place name, it is perhaps the same as the Souian *Sugari*, meaning "stingy" or "spoiled people" or "of-the-river-whose-water-cannot-be-drunk." Thought to be on the upper Carolina coast in the 1500s, the tribe moved frequently and the last record of them in historic times is with the Eno in North Carolina. (see FRANCISCO OF CHICORA)

CHICORA, FRANCISCO OF – In 1521, Spaniards sailing out of Santo Domingo landed near Georgetown to explore the region for possible future settlement. Here, they met a tribe of friendly Indians who they invited aboard ship under the guise of providing them with food, European clothes, and various trinkets. As soon as the Indians were aboard, the Spanish set sail, carrying the Indians to Santo Domingo, where they were sold as slaves. Among them was a man who became known as Francisco of Chicora, owned by the Spanish court historian Peter Martyr. He recounted stories of his homeland, Chicora, providing details about tribal names, customs, and religious practices. Peter Martyr recorded this information in one of the first great histories of the New World, *De Orbo Novo*, which provides the earliest written record of the eastern Siouan peoples. In 1525, the Spanish sent a new expedition to Carolina, bringing Francisco of Chicora and several other Indians along as interpreters. As soon as the ships made landfall, the Indians disappeared into the forest. After four years as a slave in Santo Domingo, Francisco of Chicora was home.

CHICORA RIFLES – Established during Reconstruction, the Chicora Rifles was a company formed from the MOUNT PLEASANT town militia. During the Spanish-American War, they became the Chicora Company of the South Carolina Naval Militia, under the command of Lieutenant R.H. PINCKNEY.

CHIGGER – Common name for the red bug (family *Trombiculidae*), a six-legged biting insect that leaves a large, itching welt. The name comes from the African word *jiga*, which means "insect." (see GULLAH)

CHILDSBURY – Also spelled *Childsberry* and known as Strawberry, this community on the eastern side of the WEST BRANCH of the COOPER RIVER was first granted to colonist James Childs in 1698. In 1706, Childs laid out a town, which, during its peak (1720–1770) contained a tavern, school, tannery, LUMBER yard, BRICKYARD, shops, and perhaps a small fortification since, at that time, the town was on the edge of the frontier. Here also was the STRAWBERRY FERRY crossing the Cooper River. At his death in 1720, Childs's will provided land for a church and a burying place for the town's inhabitants. In 1725, the CHAPEL OF EASE called STRAWBERRY CHAPEL was erected. Each May and October, fairs were held at Childsbury. A notice in a 1752 *Gazette* announced that at the "Childsberry Fair at Strawberry" there would be "a hoop-petticoat to be run for by two ladies," as well as "a pudding and role of tobacco to be grinn'd for by six men." A nearby racetrack held regular horse races. After the 1770s, the town disappeared. The town site is on the National Historic Register. (see STRAWBERRY CHAPEL, STRAWBERRY FERRY)

CHRIST CHURCH PARISH – Created by the CHURCH ACT of 1706, the name given to the area east of the COOPER RIVER, later named MOUNT PLEASANT. In 1712, the Reverend Gilbert Jones described the parish as being "36 miles in length from George Haddrell's Plantation on Charleston harbor to Joseph Wigfall's cowpen at head of Wando River; 7 miles in width from George Logan's Plantation on Wando River to Jonathan Perry's plantation on the coast." Christ Church was first erected as a small wooden building in 1707. Burned accidentally in 1725, it was rebuilt of brick in 1726. During the REVOLUTIONARY WAR, the British burned it in 1782. With only the walls remaining, the church was again rebuilt, only to be destroyed by Union troops during the CIVIL WAR. It was restored in 1874 and has since served an active Protestant Episcopal congregation.

CHURCH ACT – On November 30, 1706, an act divided the Province of South Carolina into ten defined parishes to serve as both political and religious entities. Charleston peninsula was named St. Philip's Parish; Colleton County was divided into St. Paul's and St. Bartholomew's. BERKELEY COUNTY was divided into six parishes, CHRIST CHURCH, ST. THOMAS PARISH (later ST. THOMAS & ST. DENIS), ST. JOHN'S PARISH, BERKELEY (Upper and Lower), St. James Goose Creek, and St. Andrew's. The French settlement on the SANTEE RIVER in Craven County was named ST. JAMES SANTEE. This parish system was borrowed entirely from the BARBADOS system of parish divisions.

CIVIL WAR – The EAST COOPER area had the marked distinction of being directly involved with the first shots fired during this war, and both FORT SUMTER and FORT MOULTRIE played an integral role in the defense of Charleston throughout the entire four years of conflict. The crew of the Confederate submarine H.L. *HUNLEY* also trained in MOUNT PLEASANT and on SULLIVAN'S ISLAND, and it was from BREACH INLET that the *Hunley* left to attack the U.S.S. *HOUSATONIC*. A CONFEDERATE LINE of breastworks stretched from the WANDO RIVER at BOONE HALL to the seacoast mainland at COPAHEE SOUND. Other defenses included BATTERY GARY (near the present OLD BRIDGE) and smaller defenses at HOG ISLAND,

HOBCAW POINT, and HADDRELL'S POINT, and batteries at Kinloch's Landing and Venning's Landing, both off present-day RIFLE RANGE ROAD. During the summer of 1863, following the fierce action at Battery Wagner on Morris Island, two hospitals were established in Mount Pleasant to care for the wounded. Outside of the intense activity near the harbor, the East Cooper area saw little action until early 1865. GENERAL SHERMAN, having decided to march his army to Columbia, ordered a fleet of ships into BULL'S BAY, a feint to make it appear that he was planning a direct attack on Charleston. In early February, a large contingency of Federal gunboats and other armed vessels under the command of General Edward E. POTTER arrived at Bull's Bay and, after a week of reconnoitering, decided upon landing on the shoreline at SEWEE BAY near the summer community at ANDERSONVILLE. Confederate troops quickly responded by manning the CONFEDERATE LINE at CHRIST CHURCH and also batteries at Buck Hall Plantation on the north shore of AWENDAW Creek. Other than some brief shelling between the Federal gunboats and the Confederate battery at Andersonville, no direct combat ensued. Instead, discovering Sherman's true intent and faced with an extreme shortage of troops in South Carolina, the order came to evacuate Charleston and the troops were ordered to meet the enemy in the midlands. On February 17, 1865, after four years of almost unceasing bombardments, Fort Sumter and Fort Moultrie were abandoned and Federal troops entered Charleston unopposed. Mount Pleasant was for a time under the command of General JAMES BEECHER. It was during this period that many of the outlying plantations were plundered and many of the houses burned. The Union foraging group known as POTTER'S RAIDERS also besieged the countryside during this period. (see Major Robert ANDERSON, ANDERSONVILLE, BATTERIES & FORTIFICATIONS, GENERAL PIERRE BEAUREGARD, General JAMES BEECHER, BLOCKADE RUNNING, CAPE ROMAIN, CASTLE PINCKNEY, CHRIST CHURCH PARISH, *CELT*, *COFFEE*, CONFEDERATE CEMETERY, CAPTAIN N.L. COSTE, ABNER DOUBLEDAY, GRACE-CHURCH, JONES SHIPYARD, LIMERICK, MOULTRIEVILLE, *PLANTER*, GENERAL SHERMAN, SPANISH MOSS, SWASH CHANNEL, WAPPETAW, WHILDEN)

CLEMENT'S FERRY – This ferry crossed the COOPER RIVER from DANIEL ISLAND at CLOUTER CREEK to Charleston Neck, known formerly as SCOTT'S FERRY. John Clement was born *c*. 1685 in CAROLINA; his son John was invested with the ferry in the 1790s. In 1792, an act gave John Clement permission to erect a bridge over Clouter's Creek, "provided the same shall not impede the navigation of boats and vessels going through the same." William Clement received investiture of the ferry in 1801 and in 1810. In the mid-1700s, the ferry became familiarly known as the CALAIS ferry for the large number of French HUGUENOTS and their descendants who lived on this side of the river. (see CALAIS AND DOVER, LESESNE)

CLEMENT'S FERRY ROAD – Name of the main road leading from CAINHOY across DANIEL ISLAND to the western side of THOMAS ISLAND on the COOPER RIVER. The road takes its name from the ferry invested to John Clement in the 1790s. The road dates to 1712, when an act was passed "to make a Highway or Common Road upon Thomas Island on the NW Side of Wando River." This act also required residents " . . . to keep in good and sufficient repair the Bridge over the Creek on the NW side of Thomas Island commonly called the WADING PLACE, and to reimburse Robert Daniel Jr. who built and erected the bridge." (see WADING PLACE)

CLINTON, SIR HENRY (1738–1795) – Commander of the British forces that attacked Fort Sullivan on June 28, 1776. Greatly outgunning the Americans with over 50 warships offshore and having landed 2,500 foot soldiers on LONG ISLAND (now ISLE OF PALMS), Clinton, with Admiral Sir Peter Parker, was certain of an easy victory. The eventual defeat by WILLIAM MOULTRIE at Fort Sullivan became an embarrassment that caused Clinton to later write volumes in his own defense. (see REVOLUTIONARY WAR)

CLOUTER CREEK – On the west side of THOMAS ISLAND, this deepwater creek was named for early settler Thomas Clouter, described as "freeman, mariner, Captain and gentleman." He received his first grant for 200 acres "on Cooper River" in October 1679, and a second for an additional 360 acres in July 1682. In 1760, "Clowter's Plantation," then owned by Richard Beresford Jr., was put up for sale and described as being 420 acres, 9 miles from town, "upon a bold creek, and has a tolerable good dwelling house."

COAST GUARD STATION – On SULLIVAN'S ISLAND at Station 18 behind the SULLIVAN'S ISLAND LIGHTHOUSE. This was the oldest lifesaving station in South Carolina. The boathouse and administration building were constructed in the Eastlake style, c. 1891. The earthen bunker between the lighthouse and administration building is a remnant of the Spanish-American War, c. 1898. The lighthouse was erected in 1962. The Coast Guard Station was decommissioned in 1973. (see SULLIVAN'S ISLAND LIGHTHOUSE)

COASTAL WATCH – In the late 1600s and early 1700s, watches were set on almost all of the remote barrier islands along the Carolina coast. These lookouts were crude affairs, roughly made wooden towers from which they could fire a cannon or light a beacon to warn of approaching vessels, usually manned by "one white man and two Indians." FLORENCE O'SULLIVAN had the lookout on SULLIVAN'S ISLAND in 1674. In 1690, three men were on Sullivan's Island, given the charge of making "one or more fires, as they shall think convenient for the acquainting of the Towne of the number of any ship or ships . . . that may appear." On LONG ISLAND (now ISLE OF PALMS), it was ordered that "two white men and two Indians and one canoe" be posted at each end of the island. In

1707, Benjamin Webb oversaw the watch at BULL'S ISLAND, consisting of "one white man and two Seewee or neighboring Indians." In 1717, Captain William Capers was in charge of the Bull's Island watch. (see LOOKOUT TOWER ON SULLIVAN'S ISLAND)

COFFEE, G.W. – A steam-driven ferry serving SULLIVAN'S ISLAND and MOUNT PLEASANT from Charleston in the 1800s. During the CIVIL WAR, it was converted into a Confederate BLOCKADE RUNNER.

COINBOW CREEK – An early name for WAKENDAW CREEK, also spelled Cornbow. The name likely is Native American, meaning unknown. In 1703, John White had a warrant for 200 acres "bounding Easterly and Southerly on Coinbow Creek alias Wakendaw Creek being part of a greater parcel of Land formerly Granted to Rich'd Rowser."

COLEMAN BOULEVARD – This main thoroughfare through MOUNT PLEASANT was named in honor of Mount Pleasant Mayor Francis F. Coleman, who served from 1946 to 1960.

COLLETON, JOHN, JAMES, & THOMAS – From BARBADOS, these three members of the Colleton family played significant roles in the founding of the CAROLINA colony. Sir John Colleton was one of the original LORDS PROPRIETORS and the first to suggest the idea of establishing the colony to LORD ANTHONY ASHLEY COOPER. Thomas Colleton was made a landgrave in the colony. James Colleton served as proprietary governor from 1686 to 1690. Colleton County to the south of Charleston retains the name. (see BARBADOS, BIGGIN, CAROLINA, CHURCH ACT, CYPRESS BARONY, LORDS PROPRIETORS, MEPKIN, TIPPYCUTLAW, WADBOO)

COLLINS CREEK – A tributary of the South SANTEE RIVER, this creek was originally called WASHASHAW by the Indians. It was later named for colonial landowner Jonah Collins. John Collins (d. 1707) was from BARBADOS and was married to Elizabeth Parris, the daughter of Alexander Parris. He next married Elizabeth Cacique, the daughter of a Cherokee chief. At his death in 1707, he owned three plantations, BULL'S ISLAND, and a town lot in CHARLES TOWN. Son Jonah Collins (d. 1749) was married to Sarah Ruberry. His son Alexander inherited TIBWIN Plantation. (see AWENDAW, HOG ISLAND, HOPSEWEE, JEREMY CREEK)

COMINGTEE – This former RICE plantation is located at the point where the COOPER RIVER forms a TEE, dividing into the EAST BRANCH and the WEST BRANCH. The property was originally granted to John Coming in the late 1600s. *Comingtee* may be a combination of his name and the plantation's location at the Tee. Some have suggested that the word may also be an adaptation of *Combe-in-Tene*, an estate near Coming's home in England. At John Coming's death, his wife, Affra, inherited the property, and the property later was inherited by nephews Elias Ball and John Harleston. The plantation remained a Ball family landholding until 1918.

COMMODORE PERRY – Ferry boat serving SULLIVAN'S ISLAND, MOUNT PLEASANT, and Charleston as part of the CHARLESTON & SEASHORE RAILROAD COMPANY, *c.* 1905.

COMMON, THE – The original MOUNT PLEASANT town common was part of GREENWICH VILLAGE, developed by JONATHAN SCOTT in the 1760s. Its purpose was to provide all residents with a common place to gather firewood. In 1889, The Common was divided into lots for residential use. (see GREENWICH VILLAGE)

COMMON STREET – Original name of ROYALL AVENUE in Mount Pleasant's OLD VILLAGE.

CONCORD, *PACKHORSE*, and *TABAR* – British prison ships anchored in Charleston harbor in 1780–81 during the REVOLUTIONARY WAR. The ships held American prisoners taken at the battles of Camden and Charleston. Conditions were so deplorable on these ships (they were ravaged by smallpox and influenza) that within a year, 800 out the 2,100 prisoners on these ships died.

CONFEDERATE CEMETERY – This tiny cemetery is located between ROYALL AVENUE and PITT STREET in Mount Pleasant's OLD VILLAGE (on Carr Street behind the DARBY BUILDING). The cemetery contains memorials to the men from CHRIST CHURCH PARISH who died during the War of 1812 and the CIVIL WAR.

CONFEDERATE LINES – In 1861, a line of earthworks was erected to protect MOUNT PLEASANT from potential Union attack from the north. This approximately 2.5-mile-long defense extended from BOONE HALL PLANTATION across to CHRIST CHURCH and on to the seacoast mainland at HAMLIN SOUND. Built under the supervision of Lieutenant of Engineers Philip Edward PORCHER of OAKLAND PLANTATION, it was approximately 10 feet high and flanked by a water-filled ditch. Gun emplacements were spaced along the line as well. Porcher recounted to historian Anne King GREGORIE that this defense was built "with Negro labor, and that all pines along the earthwork were felled with their tops pointing northeast to deter the expected enemy." (see CIVIL WAR)

COOPER, LORD ANTHONY ASHLEY (1621–1683) – "This which is my Darling" is how Lord Anthony Ashley Cooper referred to the CAROLINA settlement. Assuming the leadership of the LORDS PROPRIETORS in 1669, with Sir JOHN COLLETON he was largely responsible for spearheading the successful settlement of Charles Town. He devised the FUNDAMENTAL CONSTITUTIONS OF CAROLINA, written with his secretary, the philosopher John Locke. The ASHLEY RIVER (originally called the KIAWAH by the Indians) and the COOPER RIVER (originally called the ETIWAN) were renamed in his honor. He later held the title of Earl of Shaftesbury.

COOPER RIVER – Originally called the ETIWAN after the Indian tribe of the same name who lived in the DANIEL ISLAND region, the river divides into two branches at the TEE, the WEST BRANCH, and the EAST BRANCH, approximately 20 miles inland. Beginning in the late 1600s, large plantations, primarily devoted to the cultivation of RICE, were erected along both shores of the river. BRICKMAKING concerns followed. In the 17th and early 18th centuries, the river was the main mode of transportation between the plantations and town. (see ABOVE THE SALTS, COMINGTEE)

COOPER RIVER BRIDGE – Finished in 1929, the original Grace Memorial Bridge was a narrow two-lane bridge that carried two-way traffic. Named in honor of John P. Grace, a past mayor of Charleston, it took approximately 600 men to build this bridge; 14 died during construction. A second, three-lane bridge, the Silas Pearman Bridge, was built in 1962. Both bridges had a vertical clearance of 135–150 feet, depending upon the span. The new bridge is named to honor South Carolina senator and OLD VILLAGE resident Arthur P. Ravenel.

COOTER – A GULLAH name for turtle, which comes from the African word *kuta*, for turtle. In the mid-20th century, Captain Robert MAGWOOD's "Cooter Pen" on SHEM CREEK once raised diamondback turtles for shipment to Northern restaurants. (see MAGWOOD, TURTLES)

COPAHEE SOUND – A marshland bay just off PORCHER'S Bluff on the MOUNT PLEASANT mainland. The name is from the Siouan word *copa*, meaning "creek."

COPPER BUOYS – From the March 5, 1753 *Gazette*: "Last Tuesday Morning the Buoys brought by Capt. Ball from London (which are now covered with Copper), were carried down in three Schooners, and placed at the Bar of the Harbor." (see CROSSING THE BAR, PILOTS)

CORDESVILLE – This crossroads community on Highway 402 above HUGER takes its name from HUGUENOT émigré Antoine Cordes (d. 1712). Cordes was in Carolina by 1685, settling at WADBOO Barony on the upper reaches of the COOPER RIVER.

CORNWALLIS, LORD CHARLES (1735–1805) – General in command of the British troops in South Carolina during the REVOLUTIONARY WAR. After the fall of Charleston, for a time he made his headquarters in MOUNT PLEASANT at the HIBBEN House. (see MOUNT PLEASANT PLANTATION)

COSTE, CAPTAIN NAPOLEON L. (*c.* 1809–1885) – In ABNER DOUBLEDAY'S book, *Reminiscences of Fort Sumter and Moultrie in 1860–61*, Doubleday writes of watching the Confederates confiscate the various Federal harbor installations. "A new outrage took place in full view of our garrison," wrote Doubleday. "The United States Revenue Cutter, which lay anchored in the stream, was turned over by its commander, Captain N.L. Coste, to the authorities of South Carolina . . . To retain this vessel was simply an act of piracy." By this action, Captain Coste provided the first vessel for the Confederate Navy. Coste had earlier captained the naturalist and artist JOHN JAMES AUDUBON on expeditions in Florida and the Gulf Coast. The family has long been associated with SULLIVAN'S ISLAND and descendants still reside on the island. (see AUDUBON, CIVIL WAR)

COTTON – This important cash crop was cultivated with moderate success during the antebellum period on plantations in the EAST COOPER area, although being smaller than those on the islands of the lower coast. The cotton grown on DANIEL ISLAND plantations as well as at BOONE HALL and other seacoast plantations was called "Sea Island Cotton," an esteemed long-staple cotton that was a major export to Europe. It was second only to rice as a money-producing crop for area planters. (see BOONE HALL, BLOCKADE RUNNING, DEWEES ISLAND, GROVE PLANTATION, LESESNE, PALMETTO GROVE)

COUNTRY FEVER – Name given to various diseases, including malaria and yellow fever, so named because people originally thought these diseases originated from the "bad air" (hence the word *malaria*) of the swampy interior lowlands. They did not yet know these diseases were transferred through mosquitoes, nor did they understand that the rice fields and reserve ponds were natural mosquito-breeding areas. They did know that a summer spent in the country could lead to illness. Consequently, planters and their families "resorted" to beach and harbor areas each summer where the air was considered more salubrious. This gave rise to the resorts of McCLELLANVILLE, the MOUNT PLEASANT harbor front, and SULLIVAN'S ISLAND. (see DISEASE, PEST HOUSE, RESORTS, STRANGER'S FEVER)

COVE, THE – Located behind the southern end of SULLIVAN'S ISLAND, The Cove afforded a sheltered anchorage for boats going to and from the island. COVE INLET (now part of the INTRACOASTAL WATERWAY) ran between MOUNT PLEASANT and the island.

COVE INLET BRIDGE – This was the original name of the OLD BRIDGE that connected MOUNT PLEASANT with SULLIVAN'S ISLAND. It was erected *c.* 1898 as a trolley bridge. (see CHARLESTON & SEASHORE RAILROAD COMPANY, LEE'S BRIDGE, OLD BRIDGE.)

CROAKER – This small saltwater fish (*Micropogon undulatus*) is a bottom feeder and easily caught from docks on tidal creeks or in the surf. "They croke [*sic*] and make a noise in your Hand," wrote JOHN LAWSON in the early 1700s, adding that they had a "shape like a Pearch, in Taste like a Whiting."

CROAKER SACK – This thick burlap bag did not get its name because it was used for carrying croaker fish, but instead was used to TOTE potatoes, onions, and other vegetables. The original sacks were made of hemp, a member of the crocus family. The GULLAH adapted "crocus sack" into "croaker sack," and the name survived. (see OYSTER ROAST)

CROSSING THE BAR – In the days of sail and prior to the building of the JETTIES, entering the harbor was a difficult and treacherous task since a line of ever-shifting shoals stretched across the harbor entrance. Harbor PILOTS were on SULLIVAN'S ISLAND as early as the 1680s to assist ships in and out of the harbor. Even with a pilot aboard, crossing the bar could be precarious, as reported in the March 5, 1753 *Gazette*: "The Snow Hereford, Capt. Peard, of and for Bristol, with a valuable Cargo, attempted to get out, the wind being very high, carried away her Fore-top mast, and was drove ashore." (see JOHN JAMES AUDUBON, COPPER BOUYS, CAPTAIN N.L. COSTE, DRUNKEN DICK'S SHOALS, JETTIES, PILOTS)

CUSABO INDIANS – Designation given by early colonists to the coastal Indian tribes who lived between Charleston and the Savannah River. They included the ETIWAN, KIAWAH, Stono, Edisto, Ashepoo, Combahee, Wimbee, and Kusso (also spelled *Coosa*). The SEWEE and WANDO, although they lived north of the harbor, were sometimes included as Cusabo. The name may be a derivative of "Coosa-boys." (see CONCISE HISTORY)

CYPRESS – The U.S.S. *Cypress* was a government boat at FORT MOULTRIE in the early 1900s. During the hurricane of August 27–28, 1911, the *Cypress* and the ferry *SAPPHO* evacuated approximately 800 people from SULLIVAN'S ISLAND and ISLE OF PALMS, who otherwise would have been stranded by the storm. Although the storm inundated both islands, there were no deaths or injuries on either island. (see HURRICANE ALLEY)

CYPRESS BARONY – Granted in 1683 to Thomas COLLETON, second son of Sir John Colleton, this BARONY on the upper portion of the Cooper River's EAST BRANCH included the plantations called LIMERICK, KENSINGTON, HYDE PARK as well as Fishbrook and Windsor.

DA or DAH – A GULLAH term for a child's nurse, the name comes from the African word *Da*, which means "nurse" or "old woman."

DANIEL ISLAND – The Indians called this island ITTIWAN, an alternative spelling of ETIWAN, and in one historical source it is referred to as MAWAN. This large, fertile island is formed by the WANDO and COOPER RIVERS, with BERESFORD CREEK forming its northern border. The island went through several name changes during the early years of colonization and was at times known as THOMAS' ISLAND before it took the name of landowner Robert Daniell in the 1680s. With its close proximity to the Charleston peninsula, grants for land on the island began as early as 1671. By 1700, the island's plantations were becoming a major supplier for CHARLES TOWN, providing LUMBER, subsistence crops, beef, and ultimately, BRICKS to the growing town. Early settlers on the island reflect the diversity of cultures in the colonial period, with both French HUGUENOTS as well as English and planters from BARBADOS and a substantial number of DISSENTERS. The island remained a thriving plantation area until the CIVIL WAR, after which many of the plantations were abandoned or fell into ruin. Beginning in the 1930s, wealthy financier Harry F. Guggenheim began purchasing land and eventually owned almost all of the island, which he kept as a retreat and an undeveloped nature preserve. The only road leading onto the island was CLEMENT'S FERRY ROAD, then a narrow road with portions still unpaved. Not until the 1980s with the building of the Mark Clark Expressway and after the Guggenheim Foundation released the island from its restrictions as a nature preserve, did the island became accessible for development.

DARBY – Captain Michael Darby (d. *c.* 1740) was in the DANIEL ISLAND region at least by 1718, when he was mentioned as an executor to the will of John McMurtry, "minister of the Gospell at Kainhoy." He served in various public capacities and represented ST. THOMAS PARISH in the first royal assembly (1721–1724). Elected to the Third Royal Assembly (1728), he refused to qualify because, as a DISSENTER, he found "swearing the oaths on the Holy Evangelists was contrary to his conscience." Darby married four times. On May 21, 1717, he married Mary Warnock, with whom he had three children: Hannah, Joseph, and Mary. His second wife, Elizabeth, died March 3, 1733. He had one child, Judith, by his third wife (name unknown), who died in November 1734. His fourth wife, Susannah, bore him a son, Michael Videau, who was born in 1739.

DARBY BOULEVARD – Named for Gordon McGrath Darby (1875–1936), who was mayor of Mount Pleasant from 1960 to 1976.

DARBY BUILDING – On PITT STREET in Mount Pleasant's OLD VILLAGE, this building erected *c.* 1884 served first as the BERKELEY COUNTY Courthouse. It later became a Lutheran Seminary and, for a time, a publishing concern. From 1919 to 1964, it was used as the First Baptist Church. The structure became Mount

Pleasant's town hall in 1978 and was later used by the town as their recreation and fine arts building.

DARRELL CREEK – In CHRIST CHURCH PARISH, a tributary of the upper WANDO RIVER. The name is a corruption of the Dorril (also variously spelled *Dorrell*) family. (see DORRELL)

DATA – Also spelled as *Dauhe*, the Native American name for the area on the WANDO RIVER on the western branch of Horlbeck Creek. In 1694, ROBERT FENWICK was granted 500 acres on the Wando River, "Knowne by ye name Data," which adjoined "Major Boon's land on the one side and to a place named Weehoy on the other side." In 1697, Nathaniel Snow had a warrant for land lying between "Dauhe and Weeho plantations." The meaning of the word is unknown. (see FENWICK, WEEHOY)

DEARSLEY'S CREEK – Early name for SHEM CREEK, after Colonel George Dearsley, colonist from BARBADOS with his father, Richard Dearsley. Both were among the first to have land grants east of the COOPER RIVER. George Dearsley owned most of the land from Shem Creek to HOBCAW in the late 1600s and early 1700s, as well as land at BOWATT. His lands at WAPPETAW were left to his son, Edward, when Dearsley died in 1716. (see BOWATT, HAMLIN SOUND, OAKLAND PLANTATION, BENJAMIN QUELCH, YOUGHALL PLANTATION)

DEER – So plentiful were deer in early Carolina that trading with the Indians for the skins of deer and other animals was one of the earliest, most profitable, and longest commercial ventures of the Carolina colony. Between 1699 and 1715, the average export of deerskins to Europe from Carolina was 54,000 skins a year; in 1706, 121,355 skins; in 1731, 250,000 skins. In 1748, the colony exported an estimated 600,000 deerskins. (see CONCISE HISTORY)

DEWEES ISLAND – A barrier island between ISLE OF PALMS and CAPERS ISLAND, it was one of the HUNTING ISLANDS of the SEWEE, who called the island TIMICAU. Originally granted to Colonel Thomas Cary in 1697, by the mid-1700s, the island was owned by Cornelius Dewees (1719–1796), who erected a shipyard on the island that specialized in building brigantines. Wood from the island was also used in the construction of Fort Sullivan. During the War of 1812, British troops landed on the island in August 1813, and burned the island plantations. In the 1840s, it belonged to the Deliesseline family. Today, Dewees is a privately owned, restricted residential development, accessible only by boat.

DISEASE – "Disease malignant fills the Air . . . " began a poem in the *Gazette* on July 12, 1760, of the disastrous smallpox epidemic where over 6,000 people contracted the disease and more than 700 died. Disease was perhaps the most feared element of colonial life during the colony's early years. Reverend Hugh Adams, one of the first to serve the CAINHOY and WAPPETAW meeting houses, wrote of the 1698 smallpox epidemic, "The dead were carried in carts, being heaped one upon another. Worse by far than the Great Plague of London, considering the smallness of the town. Shops shut up for six weeks; nothing but carrying medicines, digging graves, carting the dead." Medicine was rudimentary and the causes unknown. It was understood, however, that some diseases were being imported into the colony. In 1707, a LAZARETTO, more commonly known as the PEST HOUSE, was built on Sullivan's Island to quarantine immigrants, particularly the slaves brought from Africa, as a proactive step to keep epidemics from entering the colony. Another broad term for disease was COUNTRY FEVER, since they considered the air in the swampy interior lowlands as being the cause of the malarial fevers that arose during the summer months. Planters soon began "resorting" to places they considered healthier, such as SULLIVAN'S ISLAND and harbor front MOUNT PLEASANT. (see FRENCH-SPANISH INVASION, RESORTS, STRANGER'S FEVER)

DISSENTERS – Term given to the early Protestants who worshipped outside of the Church of England. These included Quakers, Congregationalists, Presbyterians, Anabaptists, and the French Protestants called HUGUENOTS. As the FUNDAMENTAL CONSTITUTIONS OF CAROLINA ensured freedom of worship for all religious sects, a significant number of colonists came to the colony for religious reasons. The WAPPETAW and CAINHOY meeting houses both began as houses of worship for Congregationalist dissenters. Dissenters soon made up almost one-half of the total population of the colony. They became powerful politically, so much so that a group of English and Barbadian colonists, the Goose Creek Men, spurred into legislation the Exclusion Act, which required that anyone serving in public office must show proof of being an Anglican communicant. Emissaries were sent to England in 1706 to speak with Queen Anne, who declared the Exclusion Act void and an "abuse of the charter." Interestingly, the written plea to Queen Anne was authored by Daniel Defoe, author of *Robinson Crusoe* and *Moll Flanders*. (see CAINHOY MEETING HOUSE, DARBY, FUNDAMENTAL CONSTITUTIONS, HUGUENOTS, VENNING, WAPPETAW, WHILDEN)

DORRELL – This name has been spelled variously as *Darrell*, *Dorrell*, and *Dorrill*. Members of the family owned plantations from the WANDO RIVER at DARRELL CREEK to the seacoast. The union of Robert Dorrell Sr. and Elizabeth Cook in 1736 produced seven children, including Robert (1737–66), John (b. 1740), Jonathan (1745–88), Joseph, and William. Subsequent marriages merged the Dorrell family with other early Christ Church families, particularly the Whitesides family. Jonathan Dorrell married Mary Whitesides; his brother William married her sister, Elizabeth. When Robert Dorrell died in 1766, his widow married John Whitesides. These unions not only unified the families, but their landholdings as well. During the REVOLUTIONARY WAR, Captain (later

Major) Joseph Dorrell served with General WILLIAM MOULTRIE at the Battle of Fort Sullivan.

DOUBLEDAY, ABNER (1819–1893) – Reputedly invented the game of baseball, Doubleday was second in command under Major ROBERT ANDERSON at FORT SUMTER at the outset of the CIVIL WAR. Doubleday is credited with firing the first return shot against the Confederates from Fort Sumter. He also aimed a barrage at the MOULTRIE HOUSE, the grand hotel on SULLIVAN'S ISLAND, at the outbreak of the war. (see CAPTAIN N.L. COSTE, CIVIL WAR, MOULTRIE HOUSE)

DOVER FERRY – With CALAIS FERRY on DANIEL ISLAND, the name given to the Charleston Neck landing site of the ferry crossing on the COOPER RIVER. The name was a humorous reference to the Calais to Dover ferry in the English Channel. (see CALAIS & DOVER FERRY)

DRUNKEN DICK'S SHOALS – This shallow sand shoal between the JETTIES and the harbor end of SULLIVAN'S ISLAND has been so named since the 1800s. Its proximity to the mouth of Charleston harbor made it a significant marine hazard. The June 29, 1842 *Southern Patriot* reported, "The fine brig 'Gen Sumter' ashore on Drunken Dick, has bilged, and will be lost." On April 7, 1846, Charleston diarist Jacob Schirmer wrote, "Pilot Boat Water Witch lost on Drunken Dick Shoals." The origin of the name presumes that at some point in history, someone named Dick went aground here in a state of inebriation. The exact source of the name is unknown. (see CROSSING THE BAR, PILOTS)

EARTHQUAKE – On August 31, 1886, an earthquake purportedly stronger than the great San Francisco earthquake hit Charleston, causing damage to every building in the city. The shocks from this powerful tremor were felt as far away as Chicago. Small fissures filled with ejected mud and water erupted throughout MOUNT PLEASANT. On SULLIVAN'S ISLAND, mounds of sand arose, filled with water. The 1886 earthquake was not the only to affect Charleston. Other tremors occurred in 1698, 1754, 1755, 1757, 1799, 1812, and 1860. A fault line, sometimes referred to as the Summerville fault, runs generally along the ASHLEY RIVER.

EAST BRANCH, COOPER RIVER – Approximately 20 miles inland, the Cooper River divides at THE TEE, forming two distinct branches, the East Branch and the WEST BRANCH. The East Branch has its headwaters above Huger's Bridge in HELL HOLE SWAMP. As the water here is beyond the salinity point but still tidally influenced, beginning in the late 1600s, plantations were built all along the East Branch primarily given to the production of RICE. The French HUGUENOT settlement called the ORANGE QUARTER was also here at FRENCH QUARTER CREEK. The major plantations along the East

Branch's eastern shore in the parish of ST. THOMAS were The Hagan, THE BLESSING, HALIDON HILL, MIDDLEBURG, LONGWOOD, QUINBY, and SILK HOPE. POMPION HILL Chapel and ST. THOMAS CHURCH were also located on the eastern shore. Plantations on the western shore included LIMERICK, KENSINGTON, HYDE PARK, BOSSIS, RICHMOND, and BONNEAU FERRY. (see ABOVE THE SALTS)

EAST OF THE COOPER – Designation given to the lands situated east of the COOPER RIVER. This area generally includes MOUNT PLEASANT and CHRIST CHURCH PARISH, DANIEL ISLAND, the CAINHOY peninsula, the area along the EAST BRANCH of the Cooper, the upper WANDO RIVER region of WAPPETAW and farther north, McCLELLANVILLE, and the South SANTEE RIVER basin.

ECHAW – Also variously spelled as *Itshaw*, *Etchew*, and *Itchaw*, the creek and swamp on the south side of the SANTEE RIVER just above McCLELLANVILLE. In 1714, the first ST. JAMES SANTEE church was erected "in one quarter of said Parish commonly called Itshaw." The swampy, tidally influenced area was excellent for RICE, and early planters included French HUGUENOT settlers Noah Serré, Daniel HUGER, Jacob Guerard, and Elias Horry, among others. The name is of Native American origin, meaning unknown. (see JAMESTOWN, HAMPTON PLANTATION, ST. JAMES SANTEE)

EDICT OF NANTES – This decree, issued in 1598 by Henry IV of France, guaranteed a large measure of religious freedom to French Protestants, also called HUGUENOTS. On October 18, 1685, however, Louis XIV formally revoked the Edict of Nantes, renouncing all civil and religious rights of French Protestants. Thus followed a bloody period of persecution against the Huguenots. This resulted in a mass exodus (estimated at more than 400,000) of Huguenots forced to flee France for their lives. They went to England, other parts of Europe, and, ultimately, CAROLINA. (see FRENCH QUARTER, HUGUENOTS, ST. JAMES SANTEE)

EGYPT PLANTATION – Owned by Andrew HIBBEN, an intendant of MOUNT PLEASANT PLANTATION (*c.* 1854) and one of the commissioners who laid out the town in 1837, Egypt Plantation was located north of LONG POINT on the WANDO RIVER. This area, near present-day Snowden, is still referred to as the Egypt Community.

ELBOW TAVERN – A tavern at TWENTY-ONE MILE on the old GEORGETOWN ROAD; for many years this was a mustering place for the local militia. (see GEORGETOWN ROAD, INNS & TAVERNS)

ELM GROVE – Plantation in CHRIST CHURCH PARISH, situated across the GEORGETOWN ROAD from WHITEHALL and adjacent to LAUREL

HILL. Its northeastern border was on DARRELL CREEK. This was a Legare family landholding *c.* 1812–60. There was also a small BRICKYARD on the plantation that operated perhaps two to three months a year.

ENTERPRISE – Steam ferry serving SULLIVAN'S ISLAND, *c.* 1816. On September 17, 1816, the *Gazette* reported a "Melancholy Occurrence," writing of how lightning struck the *Enterprise* just as she left the Sullivan's Island landing for town. The lightning bolt " . . . descended down the chimney, and occasioned the bursting of one of her boilers. Ten persons, who were below at the time, drying themselves at the fire, were most dreadfully scalded."

ERCKMANN STREET – Street in Mount Pleasant's OLD VILLAGE, named for William E. Erckmann, mayor of Mount Pleasant from 1934 to 1946.

ETIWAN – Also spelled ITTIWAN, this Native American tribe of the Muskhogean linguistic group lived on the COOPER RIVER near its junction with the WANDO RIVER and on DANIEL ISLAND. The Cooper River's original name was Etiwan River. They may, with the WANDO, have been part of the KIAWAH tribe. In 1715, their total population was given as 240. (see CONCISE HISTORY)

ETIWAN – Ferry boat under Captain Sassard, running from Magwood's North Wharf in Charleston to SULLIVAN'S ISLAND in the 1840s.

FACTORY STREET – This street (now a part of Live Oak Drive) in Mount Pleasant's OLD VILLAGE was so named for John Hamlin's BUCKET FACTORY. (see SHEM CREEK)

FENWICK, ROBERT (d. 1724 or 1726) – The son of Robert and Anne Culcheth Fenwick of County Cumberland, England, Fenwick was one of the "Red Sea Men," arriving in CHARLES TOWN in April 1692 on the privateer *Loyall Jamaica*. Ordered away, the ship ran aground at SEWEE Bay. After posting a bond of £500 sterling and a promise that he would not leave the province, Fenwick decided to give up privateering and settle here. Fenwick apparently made the transfer from privateer to law-abiding citizen and is listed among the early Congregationalist DISSENTERS in Charleston. In 1694, he was granted 500 acres on the WANDO RIVER in the area called DATA above Horlbeck Creek. He eventually owned more than 8,000 acres of land. With his brother, John, he was a commissioner of Indian trade and served as a delegate to various assemblies. His wife, Sarah, was the daughter of Theophilus Patey, an early settler in CHRIST CHURCH PARISH. After her death in 1726/7, her will bequeathed monies to the dissenting meeting houses at CAINHOY and WAPPETAW. (see DATA, WEEHOY)

FERRY STREET – This street leading to the harbor in Mount Pleasant's OLD VILLAGE near ALHAMBRA HALL is where JUGNOT & HILLIARD and, later, H.L.P. McCORMICK, had the ferry house and dock.

FIFTEEN-MILE ROAD – On the Old GEORGETOWN ROAD and so named because it was 15 miles from the HOBCAW Ferry, this road leads to the old WAPPETAW Landing. This was the site of the WAPPETAW MEETING HOUSE. Also near here was the SIXTEEN-MILE HOUSE inn. (see INNS & TAVERNS, REVOLUTIONARY WAR)

FLAG STREET – This one-block street on SULLIVAN'S ISLAND leading from the grounds of the COAST GUARD STATION to Station 18½, was so named for the flagstaff that once stood at the Coast Guard Station (approximately where the lighthouse now stands).

FOGARTIE (FORGARTY) CREEK – In 1681, Edmund Fogartie was granted 400 acres near CAINHOY, "being upon Wandoe Creek and being upon the Mulberrie point." A 1709 act to establish roads noted, "that all male persons, as far as the house of John Fogertie, inclusive, shall be liable . . . towards the making, reparation and mending of the highway, paths and bridges aforesaid, from the house of Colonel Robert Daniell, on Thomas's Island . . . to the house of the said Fogartie." It also gives reference to "all male persons above sixteen years of age inhabiting on the north-east side of Canhaw Bridge, as far as the plantation of John Fogertie." In the 1750s, the CAINHOY FERRY was under the care of descendant Joseph Fogartie. Stephen Fogartie married Martha Dutarque in 1783. Still standing in CAINHOY village is the Lewis Fogartie house, erected *c.* 1798. It was for Lewis Fogartie that a portion of the Cainhoy village became known as LEWISVILLE, sometimes spelled *Louisville*, in the late 1700s. The "Cainhoy Bridge" mentioned in 1709 was undoubtedly a small bridge crossing what is now Fogartie Creek. Hannah and James Fogartie had a BRICKYARD here in the 18th century.

FOLLY – The word "folly" is an archaic English term for a lush and overgrown area of bushes and trees, likely derived from the French *la feuille*, meaning "leaf." Folly Island, was so named, as was SHUTE'S FOLLY, where CASTLE PINCKNEY was located.

FORT MOULTRIE – Originally built in 1776 as Fort Sullivan, there have been three Fort Moultries at the southern point of SULLIVAN'S ISLAND. The first was built of palmetto logs and sand under the command of Colonel (later General) WILLIAM MOULTRIE. This fort was washed away by the hurricane of 1783. A second fort, built in 1796–98, was a five-sided enclosed fort, surrounded by an 8-foot ditch. During the British occupation in 1780, the fort was renamed FORT ARBUTHNOT. The fort was almost completely destroyed by the hurricane of

1804. The third Fort Moultrie was begun in 1808 and is the fort seen standing today. The fort was strengthened during the War of 1812 and the CIVIL WAR. Severely damaged during the Civil War, it was rebuilt in 1876 with further modification in the early 1900s as part of the Endicott System of coastal defenses. During World War I, Fort Moultrie had barracks for 3,000 men. In the period between the World Wars, Fort Moultrie was a major training area for the National Guard. During World War II, Fort Moultrie was again modernized, adding new batteries of heavy artillery surrounded with a shell of reinforced concrete and earth. The fort remained active until 1947; it became part of the National Park Service in 1960. (see BATTERIES & FORTIFICATIONS, CONCISE HISTORY; also MAJOR ROBERT ANDERSON, BEAUREGARD, CIVIL WAR, WILLIAM MOULTRIE, OSCEOLA, EDGAR ALLAN POE, REVOLUTIONARY WAR, GENERAL SHERMAN, SULLIVAN'S ISLAND)

FORT SUMTER – Built on a sandbar in the center of the entrance to Charleston harbor, the fort was named to honor REVOLUTIONARY WAR patriot General Thomas Sumter. Fort Sumter was begun in 1829. When the fort was garrisoned by MAJOR ROBERT ANDERSON, it was still only 90 percent complete. The fort, originally a three-tiered structure standing 50 feet above the water, was all but demolished from repeated bombardments during the CIVIL WAR. In the 1870s, repairs were made and the fort was re-armed. In 1898, BATTERY HUGER was built within the fort, a reinforced concrete fortification with an armament of 12-inch breech-loading guns. The fort remained in active service until the close of World War II. Now a national monument, it is open to the public under the auspices of the National Park Service. (see BATTERIES & FORTIFICATIONS, CONCISE HISTORY; also MAJOR ROBERT ANDERSON, CIVIL WAR, ABNER DOUBLEDAY)

FOUR-MILE ROAD – So named because it was 4 miles from the HOBCAW Ferry on the old GEORGETOWN ROAD, now VENNING Road.

FRENCH PROTESTANTS – Also called HUGUENOTS. Between 1680 and 1688, an estimated 450 French Huguenots emigrated to CAROLINA following the revocation of the EDICT OF NANTES. The first Huguenots arrived on the British naval vessel *Richmond* on April 30, 1680. They eventually established large plantations on the South SANTEE RIVER at JAMESTOWN and on the Cooper River's EAST BRANCH. (see FRENCH SANTEE, FRENCH QUARTER, HUGUENOTS, ORANGE QUARTER)

FRENCH QUARTER – Also known as the ORANGE QUARTER, this was an area in ST. THOMAS PARISH on the eastern shore of the Cooper River's EAST BRANCH that was settled in the late 1600s by French HUGUENOTS. It was here that the French church called ST. DENIS was erected. (see ORANGE QUARTER)

FRENCH QUARTER CREEK – A tributary of the Cooper River's EAST BRANCH, so named for the FRENCH QUARTER. DR. JOHN IRVING described the creek as "a stream bold enough for a vessel carrying 120 barrels of rice, to penetrate as far as Spring Hill Landing, about five miles. This creek was formerly navigable much higher up . . . but it was stopt up by Mr. [Thomas] Darrington, who threw a dam across it, substituting a canal which he dug a mile and a half in length." The Native American name for this creek was WISBOO, meaning unknown.

FRENCH SANTEE – Name given to the early HUGUENOT settlements along the South SANTEE RIVER near JAMESTOWN. The Gaillard, Gendron, Horry, HUGER, Jerman, MANIGAULT, and RAVENEL families were among those to settle in the area. In 1701, JOHN LAWSON visited this area, and while no town as such existed, he mentions the French "coming from their church," likely services held in a private home. Lawson also noted, "The French, being a temperate and industrious people . . . live like one family and each one rejoices in the prosperity and elevation of his brethren." Life was not easy for these original émigrés, as noted in a letter written to kinsmen in France by Anne, the wife of émigré Pierre Manigault: "After our arrival in Carolina, we suffered every kind of evil . . . since leaving France we had experienced every kind of affliction—disease—pestilence—famine—poverty—hard labor. I have been for six months together without tasting bread, working the ground like a slave . . . God has done great things for us . . . to bear up under so many trials." (see GERMANTOWN, HAMPTON PLANTATION, JAMESTOWN, WADMACON, WAMBAW)

FRENCH-SPANISH INVASION – In August 1706, with England at war with France and Spain, five ships carrying French and Spanish soldiers preparing to invade CHARLES TOWN were sighted by the LOOKOUT TOWER on SULLIVAN'S ISLAND. Already besieged by an epidemic of yellow fever, the timing could not have been worse for the small colony. Governor Nathaniel Johnson hurried to town from his plantation, SILK HOPE, on the Cooper River's EAST BRANCH and immediately ordered the few able-bodied men not sick with fever to march in close quarters so it would appear to the ships that the town had a strong militia. The ruse worked. Instead of attacking Charleston directly, the enemy split into small units, one group coming ashore at DEARSLEY'S CREEK (SHEM CREEK) and another came ashore near present-day Six-Mile Road, on a marsh island that later became known as OLD FORT or OLD PALMETTO FORT. With the help of the SEWEE Indians, the enemy was successfully routed. Prisoners were taken, and some 30 to 40 of the enemy were killed.

FUNDAMENTAL CONSTITUTIONS OF CAROLINA – Written by LORD ANTHONY ASHLEY COOPER with celebrated philosopher John Locke, this document outlined the doctrines and governmental policies for the CAROLINA settlement. It provided for a colonial governor, a grand council, and an elected parliament.

It also provided a rare guarantee in the 17th century: the right to worship in the religion of one's choice. (see DISSENTERS, FRENCH PROTESTANTS, HUGUENOTS)

GEORGETOWN – Located approximately 60 miles north of MOUNT PLEASANT on the Sampit River at WINYAH BAY, Georgetown was founded in 1729 by Elisha Screven. With many tidally influenced but fresh rivers in the region (the Waccamaw, Black, Pee Dee, and SANTEE Rivers), Georgetown became one of the largest RICE-producing areas in the nation. (see PETER HORRY)

GEORGETOWN ROAD – This route, built over the original Sewee Broad Path, was the main stage route from MOUNT PLEASANT to GEORGETOWN. Along the highway were INNS & TAVERNS as well as rest stops that were named for the number of miles (FOUR-MILE, Six-Mile, Eight-Mile, etc.) that they were located from the HOBCAW Ferry. At one time, mileposts were also erected along the road denoting the number of miles from the ferry. While most of the original road has been replaced by Highway 17 North, a few sections of the original road remain, still unpaved, most notably the road on which the old ST. JAMES SANTEE Church stands and the area beyond the THIRTY-TWO MILE INN at STRAIGHT REACH. (see CONCISE HISTORY)

GERMANTOWN – Community on the South SANTEE RIVER. The name is a misspelling of *Jerman*, a French HUGUENOT family with a plantation on the river in that area. In 1722, an act establishing a ferry over the SANTEE RIVER vested "the privileges and advantages" to Ralph Jerman. (see FRENCH SANTEE)

GOAT ISLAND – Located on the INTRACOASTAL WATERWAY behind ISLE OF PALMS, Goat Island received its name after the 1930s when a retired butcher from Charleston, Henry Holloway, moved to the uninhabited island with his wife, Blanche, where they lived as hermits with a herd of goats. Holloway became known as the "goat man" and, until their deaths in the 1960s, the two would often be seen on the shoreline waving to passing watercraft. Only accessible by boat, Goat Island is now sparsely populated with summer- and year-round residences. The island just to the south of Goat Island is known as Little Goat Island.

GODFREY – From BARBADOS, John Godfrey Sr. (1640–1690) and his son, Captain John Godfrey (1663–1704), both came to CAROLINA in 1670; both served as members of the Grand Council and were among the first to be granted land east of the COOPER RIVER, acquiring land at SHEM CREEK, HOBCAW, and a plantation on the Stono River. (see CONCISE HISTORY)

GOLD BUG, THE – Written by EDGAR ALLAN POE, this story of hidden pirate treasure takes place on SULLIVAN'S ISLAND, LONG ISLAND (now ISLE OF PALMS), and mainland MOUNT PLEASANT. The "gold bug" was a fictional adaptation of a *scarabaeus* (beetle) indigenous to the area. The idea for the story undoubtedly came about while Poe was stationed at FORT MOULTRIE from 1827 to 1829. Some theorize that Poe fashioned the protagonist of the story after DR. EDMUND RAVENEL. (see POE, DR. EDMUND RAVENEL)

GOOBER – Colloquial word for peanut, it is derived from the African word *guba*, meaning "peanut." (see GULLAH)

GORDON & SPRINGS FERRY – The ferry at HOBCAW, *c.* 1819. This is where PRESIDENT MONROE crossed on his visit to Charleston in 1819. (see PRESIDENT JAMES MONROE)

GRACE-CHURCH – The first Episcopal house of worship on SULLIVAN'S ISLAND at MOULTRIEVILLE. Built upon the ruins of the PEST HOUSE after the lazaretto was moved to Morris Island, Grace-Church was consecrated in 1819 and held services throughout the summer season. The church was completely destroyed by shelling during the CIVIL WAR. An 1868 report on the destruction of churches in the war, written by C.C. PINCKNEY, Peter Shand, and Paul Trapier, describes the devastation caused by bombardments, noting, "the church came in reach of their shells, which riddled roof and floor, and consumed the wood work. Its roofless walls still rise up their solemn sides in the silence of the scene." Grace-Church was never rebuilt but replaced in the early 1900s by the Church of the Holy Cross.

GRAINING – A uniquely lowcountry term for catching flounder with a spear, also called "gigging." A "grain" was the archaic Scottish word for a natural fork in a tree branch that could be fashioned into a three-pronged spear. Thus the term for stabbing flounder with a trident or a gig came to be called "graining." The term was undoubtedly brought to the lowcountry by Scottish settlers.

GRAY BAY – A large, shallow bay between GOAT ISLAND and the MOUNT PLEASANT mainland. George Gray arrived with the first colonists aboard the ship *CAROLINA* and was one of the first to settle on lands east of the COOPER RIVER. Henry Gray owned the land (later called MOUNT PLEASANT PLANTATION) prior to its purchase by Jacob MOTTE in 1749.

GRAY'S FERRY – The ferry at HADDRELL'S POINT, vested to Henry Gray in 1748. From the April 11–18, 1760 *Gazette*: "To be lett for the summer season by Jacob Motte . . . The house at the ferry, late Gray's in Christ-Church Parish."

GREENWICH VILLAGE – One of the original villages developed in the OLD VILLAGE area of MOUNT PLEASANT. In the 1760s, JONATHAN SCOTT established a typical English-style village. Within its 100-acre plat, a portion was dedicated to house lots on the waterfront and the rest designated as the town COMMON. The harbor area in front of this village was known as Greenwich Bay. Greenwich Street retains the name of this early village.

GREGORIE – The CAROLINA progenitor of this family long associated with CHRIST CHURCH PARISH was Scotsman James Gregorie (1777–1852), a prominent Charles Town merchant and planter. Gregorie's Tavern was on Bedon's Alley in CHARLES TOWN in the 1780s. He was married to Mary Hopton, daughter of merchant and planter WILLIAM HOPTON, and became an owner of WANDO PLANTATION. Gregorie descendants are affiliated through marriage with the PORCHER and VENNING families, and the Gregorie name is also associated with LAUREL HILL, MYRTLE GROVE, OAKLAND, and PORCHER's Bluff. Ferdinand Gregorie (1819–1880) was twice intendant of MOUNT PLEASANT, first in 1856–57 and again from 1874 to 1876. His granddaughter, historian Anne King Gregorie (1887–1960), was noted for her research on the SEWEE Indians and wrote the definitive history of Christ Church. (see BIBLIOGRAPHY; also CAINHOY FERRY, LEXINGTON PLANTATION, PORCHER, STARVEGUT HALL, VENNING, WANDO PLANTATION)

GRILLAGE, THE – The rocks and groins on SULLIVAN'S ISLAND on the beach in front of FORT MOULTRIE, also known as BOWMAN'S JETTY. A grillage is a framework of timbers and rocks (in this case, palmetto logs and granite) designed to act as a breakwater. Captain A.H. Bowman of the U.S. Army Corps of Engineers designed the Grillage in the 1830s and 1840s as a way to halt severe erosion on the island. (see BOWMAN'S JETTY)

GROG POND – A stop on the GEORGETOWN ROAD at Six-Mile Road. It is said that here a traveler could exchange an empty jug of grog (a mixture of rum and water) for a full, cool one. The jugs were kept cool in a nearby pond. (see INNS & TAVERNS)

GROVE PLANTATION, DANIEL ISLAND – This plantation on DANIEL ISLAND was granted in 1699 to HUGUENOT émigré Isaac LESESNE (pronounced *La-sayne*). It later was inherited by grandsons Daniel, Isaac, and Thomas Lesesne in 1784. Throughout the 18th century, The Grove supplied a thriving LUMBER business to the Charleston and shipbuilding market. During its ownership in the mid-1800s by J.P. Deveaux, it became a COTTON plantation producing almost one-third of all cotton grown in ST. THOMAS PARISH. (see LESESNE)

GROVE, THE, COOPER RIVER – This former RICE plantation on the eastern shore of the COOPER RIVER just above THOMAS ISLAND was purchased by DR. EDMUND RAVENEL in 1835. In 1852, Ravenel also added adjoining Pagett's Landing and other parts of BRABANT to The Grove lands. When scientist DR. LOUIS AGASSIZ visited Ravenel at The Grove to study freshwater fish, Ravenel had the water drained from the reserve pond so that Agassiz could more closely see the fish and their habitat—a fine step towards science but one that nearly ruined Ravenel's RICE crop. (see DR. LOUIS AGASSIZ, BRABANT, RAVENEL)

GROVE, THE, CHRIST CHURCH PARISH – This plantation on the seacoast mainland next to ANDERSONVILLE was owned by WILLIAM HORT in the late 18th century. Hort recorded in his journal: "Dined with us at the Grove, Mrs. Simons, Maria and Sarah Lydia Simons, Elias Ball, Edward Thomas and Elizabeth and Mary his daughters, Mrs. Smith, wife of Robert, Gabriel Capers and daughters, Catherine, Mary, Martha and Sarah, Rebecca and Ann Jamieson and Daniel Lesesne." This was a celebratory dinner in honor of his marriage on March 23, 1790, to Catherine Simons, the daughter of Benjamin Simons III of MIDDLEBURG Plantation. The marriage was performed at The Grove by the Reverend Robert Smith of St. Philips. The ladies in attendance were bridesmaids. (see LESESNE, MIDDLEBURG, STARVEGUT HALL)

GUERIN'S BRIDGE – This bridge over the uppermost reaches of the WANDO RIVER at WAPPETAW was first established in 1707. In 1767, an act called for the establishment of a new road and bridge, eventually known as Guerin's Bridge for the family invested with its care. The patriarch of the Guerin family in South Carolina was Vincent Guerin, a French HUGUENOT émigré from St. Nazaire, Saintonge, France. He and his descendants were among the earliest landholders in ST. THOMAS PARISH. The road leading from the bridge is now Route 98, colloquially known as Guerin's Bridge Road.

GULLAH – The term given both to the language spoken by sea island descendants of African slaves and the people themselves. Although it is an English-based language Gullah combines African dialects with elements of various European languages, with which the slaves had come into contact. In coastal Georgia, it is often used interchangeably with the term *geechie*. In Sierra Leone, the national language called Krio is similar to Gullah. Both Gullah and Krio originated in the days of the slave trade when almost the entire West African coast was studded with slave trading stations. In order to communicate with the English traders (and with each other), the Africans invented a type of pidgin English. This creole (thus the name Krio) became the *lingua franca* of the slave trade and, eventually, Sierra Leone. It was then imported into the Americas with the slaves, becoming the language we know today as Gullah. The origin of the word is still debated. Some surmise the name came from an African tribe, the Gola. It perhaps is a shortened form of Angola. Gullah has survived primarily because of the previous remoteness of the Carolina and Georgia plantations. Although diminished compared to the past, Gullah is still widely used, and many Gullah words and phrases are now permanent additions to the lowcountry lexicon. (see BIDDY, CHAINEY BRIAR, CHIGGER, COOTER, CROAKER SACK, DAH, GUMBO, JIMMIES, JOGGLING BOARD, MATHIS FERRY, NELLIEFIELD CREEK, NO-SEE-UM, POOR JOE, RICE, She Crab, SLAVERY, SWEETGRASS BASKETS, TOTE)

GUMBO – GULLAH name for a soup or stew containing okra. Gumbo is an African word for *okra*.

HADDRELL'S POINT – The point of land on the south side of SHEM CREEK where it meets the harbor. Colonist George Haddrell was granted this land in the late 1600s, and the name has remained since. At times the entire Mount Pleasant area has shown on maps as Haddrell's Point. Haddrell married Susannah Boone (1698–1759), daughter of John Boone of BOONE HALL.

HAGAN, THE – This is the first RICE plantation on the eastern shore of the COOPER RIVER's EAST BRANCH after THE TEE, first granted to Samuel Wilson in 1688. In 1722, it was owned by WILLIAM RHETT; in 1748, by Daniel HUGER. Major John Huger, son of Benjamin Huger of LIMERICK Plantation, owned the property in 1842, when it was described by DR. JOHN IRVING as having "a noble mansion and very valuable estate." (see AHAGAN)

HALIDON HILL – This former RICE plantation on the eastern shore of the Cooper River's EAST BRANCH was originally part of lands belonging to Benjamin Simons I of MIDDLEBURG. In the late 1700s and early 1800s, it became known as Hort's, when it was given to Benjamin Simons III's daughter, Catherine, and her husband, WILLIAM HORT. The name was changed to Halidon Hill in 1843 when the property was purchased by William Ball of LIMERICK Plantation. Privately owned and on the National Historic Register, the dwelling house here was originally the plantation house at QUINBY PLANTATION, moved in 1954. (see QUINBY BARONY)

HALL'S SHIPYARD – A boatyard at SHEM CREEK run by E.O. (Ned) Hall in the early part of the 20th century. Hall specialized in sailing craft, and his *Carolina*, a 25-foot "skimming dish" scow that sailed with a skipper and three crew, was a well-known racer (and winner) of turn-of-the-century regattas.

HAMLIN SOUND – This marshland bay is located off the Mount Pleasant mainland between Six-Mile Road and PORCHER'S BLUFF and named for one of the area's earliest and most enduring families. In 1696, Thomas Hamlin purchased 1,300 acres at BOWATT from George Dearsley. A warrant for land in 1702 by Captain William Capers mentions lands located "north of John Hamlin on Copahee." For three centuries, the Hamlin family has retained this land, portions of which are still actively farmed. (see BUCKET FACTORY, YOUGHALL)

HAMPTON PLANTATION – This RICE plantation on the South SANTEE RIVER in FRENCH SANTEE was the home of Daniel Horry II (d. 1785), who was married to Harriott PINCKNEY, the daughter of ELIZA LUCAS PINCKNEY. President George Washington stopped at Hampton during his

Southern Tour in 1791, entertained by Harriott Pinckney Horry and her mother;
the ladies were "arrayed in sashes and bandeaux painted with the general's portrait
and mottoes of welcome." Hampton was later the home of poet ARCHIBALD
RUTLEDGE. It is now owned by the state of South Carolina, and the house
and grounds are open to the public. (see ECHAW, ELIZA LUCAS, ST. JAMES
SANTEE, WADMACON, WAMBAW)

HAWAN – The Native American name for CAPERS ISLAND, one of the
HUNTING ISLANDS of the SEWEE.

HERON – With the storks, ibis, and egrets, a member of the order *Herodiones*.
The great blue heron (also known as a blue crane) is the largest of the American
herons, reaching a height of 4 feet. The Louisiana heron is smaller (just over 2
feet), and recognized by a slate and purplish color. The little blue heron reaches a
height of 2 feet, while the little green heron is only 18 inches tall. All feed on fish,
crabs, and other marine animals in marshland shallows.

HELL HOLE SWAMP – Local name for the large, primeval swamp stretches
(generally) from CAINHOY and HUGER eastward to JAMESTOWN and the
South SANTEE RIVER. GENERAL FRANCIS MARION and his men used
the swamp to their advantage during the REVOLUTIONARY WAR, so much
so that Marion was dubbed "the Swamp Fox." The name "Hell Hole" predates
Marion, however, and the area is named as such on William DeBrahm's map of
CAROLINA published in 1757. Dense, snaky, and ridden with alligators, it was
unquestionably inhospitable to the outsider unfamiliar with the territory. During
Prohibition, Hell Hole Swamp gained notoriety as a center for illegal trafficking in
liquor. (see BOOTLEGGING, MOONSHINE)

HIBBEN – Englishman Andrew Hibben (1728–1784) came to CAROLINA from
Kent, England, in the 1730s and soon owned considerable property, including land on
SHEM CREEK and the WANDO RIVER. James Hibben (1766–1835) purchased
MOUNT PLEASANT PLANTATION from Jacob MOTTE in 1803. Although
Motte built the original plantation house (now at 111 Hibben Street), it became
known as the Hibben Huose during James Hibben's ownership. James Hibben was a
state senator, a captain in the War of 1812, and a member of the Board of Trustees
of the South Carolina College. His son James Hibben Jr. (1799–1871) was a member
of the South Carolina House of Representatives from 1824 to 1830. Another son,
Andrew (1806–1872), of EGYPT PLANTATION served as state senator from 1848
to 1855 and was intendant of MOUNT PLEASANT *c.* 1854.

HIBBEN'S FERRY – This ferry at HADDRELL'S POINT was the first to connect
the village area of MOUNT PLEASANT with Charleston and was established *c.*
1770 by James Hibben. President George Washington crossed at Hibben's Ferry
during his visit in 1791.

JAMES HIBBEN – One of the five ferry boats owned by JUGNOT & HILLIARD, this steam-powered ferry could hold as many as 400 people. During the Civil War, the *Hibben* was converted into a Confederate BLOCKADE RUNNER.

HILLIARDSVILLE – In 1847, Oliver Hilliard and Charles Jugnot purchased a large tract of land north of the villages of GREENWICH, naming it Hilliardsville. The area near ALHAMBRA HALL was developed as a picnic ground, ferry house, and wharf. Hilliardsville was bounded by Division Street (now McCANTS DRIVE) on the west, COMMON STREET (now ROYALL AVENUE) on the north, the marsh at Cove Inlet on the south, and the harbor. (see JUGNOT & HILLARD FERRY COMPANY)

HOBCAW – Siouan for elevated way, or possibly *Hobiyaw*, meaning "far away." (see ABCAW)

HOBCAW POINT – Point of land in CHRIST CHURCH PARISH on the WANDO RIVER at its junction with the harbor. The earliest settlers considered the entire neck of land between SHEM CREEK and the Wando River as Hobcaw. David Maybank had a warrant for land at Hobcaw in 1683; George Dearsley began taking out warrants for land there in 1694. Jacob Bond was also an early landowner. In Dearsley's will, dated 1702, he mentioned ships under construction at his HOBCAW Plantation, an early record of what became known as SHIPYARD PLANTATION. The HOBCAW Ferry was the first to cross the COOPER RIVER into CHARLES TOWN, its name changing according to ownership, beginning with MATHEWS in 1700. In 1770, a brick powder magazine was erected here and guarded by the colonial militia. The area is now primarily given to residential development. (see ABCAW, *CAROLINA PACKET*, CHAINEY BRIAR, GORDON & SPRINGS FERRY, I'ON, MATHIS FERRY, MILTON'S FERRY, MOLASSES CREEK, MONROE, PEST HOUSE, PRIVATEER, BENJAMIN QUELCH, REMLEY'S POINT, REVOLUTIONARY WAR, ROSE'S SHIPYARD, SHIPYARD PLANTATION)

HOG ISLAND – Now PATRIOT'S POINT, this once large, wooded island was originally spelled *Hogg Island* and its name may have been taken from early colonist Jonathan Hogg, an early PILOT. In 1694, a grant was made to Edmund Bellinger for 17 acres ". . . on East side of Cooper River . . . commonly known as 'Hogg Island' bounding North on Hogg Island creek, South on Sullivan's Creek (SHEM CREEK) and East and West upon a marsh." The island was purchased in 1711 by Colonel Alexander Parris, who also owned SHUTE'S FOLLY (now CASTLE PINCKNEY) in Charleston harbor. Ownership next transferred to William Gibbon and Jonah Collins, then again in 1730 to Captain John Gascoigne, who renamed the island MOUNT EDGECOMBE, likely for a family estate in England. When Gascoigne sold the island in 1734, there was a house and large gardens, including fruit orchards and an ORANGE grove of more than a thousand trees. It was later owned by Andrew HIBBEN and his daughters, Elizabeth and Hannah. Over the years, Hog Island gradually began to disappear by erosion. The present land was rebuilt with dredge fill in the 1960s. (see CONCISE HISTORY; also CIVIL WAR, JONATHAN LUCAS, ORANGES, PARRIS CREEK, PATRIOT'S POINT)

HOG ISLAND CHANNEL, BATTLE OF – November 11–12, 1775, perhaps the first military engagement of the REVOLUTIONARY WAR in South Carolina. In order to keep British ships from entering the inner harbor, six hulks of vessels were ordered to be sunk in a line across the COOPER RIVER as an obstruction. When the H.M.S. *TAMAR* and *CHEROKEE* fired shots in an attempt to stop this work, they were engaged by the South Carolina ship *Defense*. The British ships retreated and the work was completed. In 1780, when Charleston was taken by the British, these sunken defense-works did not allow Admiral Arbuthnot to advance his fleet, which left open an escape route up the WANDO RIVER for the Continentals. LORD CORNWALLIS was thus ordered to head them off, which resulted in a number of skirmishes on the eastern side of the Cooper River, including the BATTLE OF BIGGIN'S BRIDGE. (see REVOLUTIONARY WAR, QUINBY BARONY, BATTLE OF VIDEAU BRIDGE, WADBOO)

HOG ISLAND HILL – The 1715 Herman Moll map of Charleston names the harbor-side area of MOUNT PLEASANT, now the OLD VILLAGE area, as "Hog Island Hill." This name undoubtedly comes from nearby HOG ISLAND. (see MOUNT PLEASANT PLANTATION)

HOPSEWEE – The Native American name for the area on the North SANTEE RIVER, meaning unknown, which became Hopsewee Plantation, first granted to John Collins in the late 1600s. In 1704, John Bell had a warrant for 500 acres "at a place called Hobshewee on ye North East Branch of Santee." It later was one of seven plantations owned by Thomas Lynch (1726–1776) and his son, Thomas Lynch Jr., a signer of the Declaration of Independence. In the early 1800s, it was in the possession of John Hume Lucas (1822–1853), the grandson of JONATHAN LUCAS. Ravaged during the Federal occupation, the plantation fell into such decline that, in 1936, Mary Doar Lucas wrote, "Now the old house is closed and has been for twenty-one years. Will it ever be opened again?" Sold to the International Paper Company in 1945, it later went through a progression of owners, and the dwelling house is now open to the public as a house museum. Hopsewee is on the National Historic Register. (see LEXINGTON PLANTATION, LYNCH'S GROVE, REVOLUTIONARY WAR, WAKENDAW, WASHASHAW)

HOPTON, WILLIAM (1710–1786) – Prominent CHARLES TOWN merchant and planter in CHRIST CHURCH PARISH. His plantations were WANDO PLANTATION and STARVEGUT HALL. His daughter Mary was married to James GREGORIE in 1789. (see BARTRAM, GREGORIE, LEXINGTON PLANTATION)

HORNED TOADS – Actually called Texas horned lizards, these 6-inch, dinosaur-like lizards are found in the dunes on SULLIVAN'S ISLAND. They are not indigenous but were likely introduced as pets by soldiers stationed at FORT MOULTRIE during World War II. Quite docile despite a ferocious appearance, they feed on insects, primarily ants.

HORRY, PETER (*c.* 1747–1815) – From the GEORGETOWN area, REVOLUTIONARY WAR patriot Peter Horry (pronounced *O-ree*) served under WILLIAM MOULTRIE during the building of the battery at HADDRELL'S POINT. He was also at the Battle of Fort Sullivan. He later described the fort as an "immense pen 500 feet long and 16 feet wide, with sand to stop the shot." He eventually earned the rank of brigadier general for his service. The Horry family in South Carolina began with French HUGUENOT émigré Elias Horry, who fled Paris and eventually settled at FRENCH SANTEE. Horry County was named for Peter Horry. (see ECHAW, HAMPTON PLANTATION, SERGEANT WILLIAM JASPER, ELIZA LUCAS, WILLIAM MOULTRIE, WADMACON, WAMBAW)

HORSESHOE CRAB – This shallow-water sea arthropod is not a true crustacean but more closely related to the spider family. One of the oldest species on earth, the horseshoe crab dates back 350 million years. Docile and slow moving, they are bottom feeders. Females are larger than males and may grow to 2 feet long, including the tail. They feed mainly on marine worms and small mollusks. The early coastal Indians used the sharp tail spike as a type of arrow point.

HORT, WILLIAM – Originally from BARBADOS, William Hort was in CAROLINA by 1772 when he married Alice Gibbs of CHRIST CHURCH PARISH. Upon her death, in 1790, he married Catharine Simons, the daughter of Benjamin Simons III of MIDDLEBURG Plantation at his GROVE Plantation on the mainland overlooking SEWEE BAY. Hort also owned HALIDON HILL Plantation, and during his ownership, it was known as Hort's. Hort served on the vestry of Christ Church in 1810. (see HALIDON HILL, THE GROVE, CHRIST CHURCH PARISH)

HOTEL SEASHORE or SEASHORE HOTEL – A hotel located on the front beach of ISLE OF PALMS at the turn of the 20th century.

HOUSATONIC, U.S.S. – Federal naval ship that was the first ever sunk by a submarine, February 17, 1864. Leaving BREACH INLET under the cover of darkness, the Confederate submarine *H.L. HUNLEY* rammed the *Housatonic* with a torpedo attached to the bow. (see CIVIL WAR, *HUNLEY*)

HUGER – This crossroads community (pronounced *U-gee*) is 10 miles north of CAINHOY on Highway 41 near the headwaters of the Cooper River's EAST BRANCH. It was named for Daniel Huger II (*c.* 1687–1754), son of

the HUGUENOT émigré, Daniel Huger, from Loudon, France, who originally
settled at FRENCH SANTEE. Huger owned a number of plantations including
LIMERICK, his permanent residence. Married to Mary Cordes, his five sons all
served with distinction during the REVOLUTIONARY WAR. Daniel III was a
delegate to the Continental Congress; John was a member of the Council of Safety,
fought under the rank of major, and later became intendant of Charleston and
secretary of state. Benjamin served in the Continental Congress, was a major with
the First Regiment of Riflemen, and was killed in action at Charleston in 1779.
Son Francis was at the Battle of Fort Sullivan and afterwards made lieutenant
colonel and quartermaster general of the Continental Army. Son Isaac became
a brigadier general. Isaac was married to Elizabeth Chalmers, daughter of DR.
LIONEL CHALMERS and Martha LOGAN of WANDO PLANTATION.
(see AHAGAN, BATTERIES & FORTIFICATIONS, BATTLE OF BIGGIN'S
BRIDGE, ECHAW, FORT MOULTRIE, HAGAN, LONGWOOD, BATTLE
OF QUINBY BRIDGE, READ, RICE HOPE, WADMACON, WAMBAW)

HUGUENOT – The name for the FRENCH PROTESTANTS escaping
religious persecution, among the earliest colonists to settle in Carolina. Huguenot
Jean Ribaut's settlement at Port Royal in 1562 was the first Protestant settlement
on American soil. Huguenots also settled in New York with the Dutch in 1614,
eventually establishing the city of New Rochelle in that state. The great Huguenot
immigration began after the Revocation of the EDICT OF NANTES. Between
1680 and 1688, more than 450 Huguenots settled in Carolina, establishing
settlements at FRENCH SANTEE and at the FRENCH QUARTER on the
EAST BRANCH of the COOPER RIVER. The Huguenot Church was one
of the first established in Charleston, c. 1681. ST. DENIS was erected on the
Cooper River's EAST BRANCH in the ORANGE QUARTER, also known as
the FRENCH QUARTER, to serve the French inhabitants there. Huguenots were
involved in both mercantile and planting endeavors, and their industriousness and
inventiveness in the culture of RICE helped make this crop become Carolina's
major export. REVOLUTIONARY WAR hero FRANCIS MARION was
of Huguenot ancestry, as was merchant and statesman HENRY LAURENS.
(see CONCISE HISTORY; also CORDESVILLE, DISSENTERS, ECHAW,
FRENCH QUARTER, FRENCH SANTEE, GERMANTOWN, GUERINS
BRIDGE, HORRY, HUGER, MANIGAULT, ORANGE QUARTER,
POMPION HILL, PORCHER, RAVENEL, ST. DENIS, BATTLE OF VIDEAU
BRIDGE, VILLEPONTOUX, WADMACON, WAMBAW)

C.S.S. *HUNLEY* – This first submarine to sink an enemy vessel was named for
Horace L. Hunley, a wealthy sugar broker from New Orleans who financed the
construction of experimental submarines for the Confederacy, called "fish boats"
and "coffin boats." Hunley brought his first submarine to Charleston in 1863. On
October 15 of that year, the boat struck bottom during a practice dive and sank,
killing everyone on board, including Hunley. Despite this setback, the Confederacy

set up a submarine school in MOUNT PLEASANT near HADDRELL'S POINT. Classroom instruction and daily exercise routines included a march on the SULLIVAN'S ISLAND beach to BATTERY MARSHALL at BREACH INLET, where their submarine, now named for its builder, was moored. Here they underwent endurance dives and submerged runs. On the night of February 17, 1864, the *Hunley*, with a crew of eight and a spar torpedo attached to her bow, left Breach Inlet to go after the U.S.S. *HOUSATONIC*, part of the Federal blockading fleet offshore. The *Hunley* rammed the *Housatonic* just forward of the mizzenmast and, following an explosion, the ship sank almost immediately. The *Hunley* retreated but never made it back to land, with all hands lost. (see CIVIL WAR)

HUNTING ISLANDS – The string of BARRIER ISLANDS stretching from Charleston harbor to BULL'S BAY used for hunting and fishing by coastal Indians, primarily the SEWEE. They included DEWEES ISLAND, which the Indians called TIMICAU; CAPERS ISLAND, known to the Sewee as HAWAN; and BULL'S ISLAND, or ONESICAU. Undoubtedly both ISLE OF PALMS and SULLIVAN'S ISLAND were similarly used by the coastal Indians, but their Native American names are not recorded.

HURRICANE – A tropical cyclone with winds more than 74 miles per hour. The word is derived from the Spanish *huracan*, adopted from the Caribbean Indian word *Juracan*. Since 1670, more than 100 hurricanes and tropical storms have hit the South Carolina shoreline with varying degrees of intensity, over one-fourth of which have been severe. (see HURRICANE ALLEY)

HYDE PARK – This former RICE plantation is on the western shore of the Cooper River's EAST BRANCH, just west of KENSINGTON. The plantation house was constructed *c.* 1798 by John Ball Sr. of KENSINGTON and still stands. An advertisement in the November 30, 1818 *Southern Patriot* noted that it contained, "115 acres of tide land, 102 acres of which is an excellent state of cultivation, 420 acres of highland, and wooded chiefly with Pine, this is also a remarkably well settled Plantation, having on it an excellent Tide Mill, which does as much execution as the most of the Mills built by Mr. Lucas, a small dwelling House, and every other building necessary for the Plantation." (see CYPRESS BARONY, JONATHAN LUCAS)

INDIGO – Sometimes written as *indico* in the 18th century, the indigo plant (*Indigofera leguminosae*) produces a blue dye. From the 1740s until the late 1790s, cakes of indigo dye became one of the lowcountry's most valuable export commodities. Indigo allowed the lowcountry planter dual use of his land—indigo was grown on high land while RICE was grown in the lowlands. It was relatively easy to grow, but extracting the dye was an extremely difficult process. The crop did not become economically successful until 1744, when ELIZA LUCAS, after a ten-year period of trial and error, finally refined the process. The plants were grown to about 3 feet when they were cut with a hook and carried to vat, covered with water and left to steep until the dye was extracted. This material was then transferred to another vat and beaten by hand until hardening. It was then cut into cakes and packaged into bags or boxes for shipment. Carolina-produced indigo dominated the world market until the 1790s. (see CONCISE HISTORY; also BRICKMAKING, LESESNE, ELIZA LUCAS, SLAVERY)

INLAND PASSAGE – Because sailing offshore could be hazardous, plantation boats and other smaller watercraft used the creeks that ran between the mainland and barrier islands to transport goods and people. This previously circuitous route was eventually straightened with the building of the INTRACOASTAL WATERWAY.

INNS & TAVERNS – Along the GEORGETOWN ROAD were numerous resting points and wayside inns where one could water horses and take refreshment. These generally were named for the number of miles that they were from the ferry landing at HOBCAW: Six Mile, Ten Mile, Sixteen Mile, and so on to the SANTEE RIVER. None of these former establishments remain. (see ELBOW TAVERN, FIFTEEN-MILE ROAD, JONES TAVERN, SIXTEEN-MILE HOUSE, TEN-MILE HOUSE, THIRTY-TWO MILE INN, WAPPETAW)

INTRACOASTAL WATERWAY – Also known as the Inland Waterway and colloquially as the "ditch." Completed in 1940, the Intracoastal Waterway extends from Maine to the Florida Keys. The Ben Sawyer Bridge to SULLIVAN'S ISLAND opens for boats using the waterway. The ISLE OF PALMS connector crosses it between GOAT ISLAND and Little Goat Island. South Carolina has 210 miles of Intracoastal Waterway. (see INLAND PASSAGE)

I'ON AVENUE – Street on SULLIVAN'S ISLAND, named for Colonel Jacob Bond I'on (1782–1859) of HOBCAW Plantation and who summered on the island in the early 1800s. Frederick Adolphus PORCHER, writing about the island in 1843, observed: "Our nearest neighbor was Colonel Jacob Bond I'on. This gentleman had been in his day a conspicuous person in the state, and still lived respected and esteemed for his sterling character. He was the last of his race. Having never married, his name would perish with him. He had been many years, I suppose all his life, a planter in Christ Church Parish, I suspect not a very successful one. He was very wealthy, had a few years before sold all his planting estates, and now resided in the summer on this Island home, in the winter in a very fine house which he had built in Charleston." Colonel I'on's house on the island was apparently a popular retreat for officers at FORT MOULTRIE, where one visitor was GENERAL WILLIAM SHERMAN, stationed at the fort after graduating from West Point. During PRESIDENT JAMES MONROE'S visit to Charleston in 1819, he was entertained at I'on's home on Sullivan's Island. Colonel I'on was affectionately known as Old Uncle by his nieces and nephews.

Porcher's diary goes on to say, "Colonel I'on's house was much resorted to by his nephew and nieces, the children of Mrs. Thomas Lowndes and of Mrs. Samuel Wragg. The latter lady was his twin sister." Porcher ends by saying, "Colonel I'on died ten years afterwards of a shocking and cruel disorder. I am told that a few days before his death one of his legs dropped off." During his lifetime, I'on owned over 1,000 acres in CHRIST CHURCH PARISH and ST. JAMES SANTEE. He is buried at the family graveyard at HOBCAW. (see HOBCAW, IRON SWAMP)

IRON SWAMP – An area of swampland in the Francis Marion National Forest between AWENDAW and HUGER near Halfway Creek. The name is a GULLAH corruption of I'on, from early landowner Jacob Bond I'on.

IRVING, JOHN BEAUFAIN (1800–1881) – This physician, RICE planter, and historian was at one time owner of three plantations on the Cooper River's EAST BRANCH, including KENSINGTON, where he made his home. Irving's writings include the history of the South Carolina Jockey Club and *A Day on the Cooper River*, a comprehensive description of the COOPER RIVER Plantations in the early 1800s. (See BIBLIOGRAPHY; also BEECHER, FRENCH QUARTER CREEK, HAGAN, WEST BRANCH)

ISLE OF PALMS – Formerly known as LONG ISLAND for its length (approximately 7 miles). The SEWEE used the island for hunting and fishing, and an early map shows a Sewee SHELL RING at BREACH INLET. In 1706, a COASTAL WATCH was erected at the north end of the island, manned by "one white man and two Sewee Indians." In 1776, SIR HENRY CLINTON landed 2,500 soldiers on the island prior to the Battle of Fort Sullivan. Their encampments lined the front beach, with one soldier writing of their "miserable situation," stating, "we have lived on nothing but salt pork and peas; we sleep on the seashore, nothing to keep us from the rains but our coats, or a miserable paltry blanket. There is nothing that grows on this paltry island, it being a mere sandbank and a few bushes which harbor millions of musketoes, a great plague that could not be worse than hell itself." During the CIVIL WAR, the island and its adjoining inlets proved ideal for Confederate BLOCKADE RUNNERS. BREACH INLET on its south end was a training ground for the Confederate submarine C.S.S. *HUNLEY*. In 1898, the island was purchased by J.S. Lawrence, who renamed it ISLE OF PALMS. Forming the CHARLESTON & SEASHORE RAILROAD COMPANY, Lawrence built a trolley bridge over Breach Inlet, and the Isle of Palms became a nationally popular summer resort. The STEEPLECHASE AMUSEMENT PARK was built on the front beach (in the same area as the present business district) and boasted a 180-foot Ferris wheel and a remarkable race course in which a field of mechanically operated iron horses and jockeys "raced" on a mechanized course to the delight of betting onlookers. There were several hotels, including the Isle of Palms Hotel, the Stag, and the SEASHORE HOTEL, all clustered around a huge pavilion with bathing houses and a boardwalk. The northernmost tip of the island is now the resort of WILD DUNES. (see CONCISE HISTORY; also BARRIER ISLANDS, COASTAL WATCHES, *CYPRESS*, *GOLD BUG*, HOTEL SEASHORE, HUNTING ISLANDS, INTRACOASTAL WATERWAY)

ITTCHICAW – Native American name for the western portion of BERESFORD CREEK on DANIEL ISLAND. In 1680, a grant was issued to Richard Codner for 76 acres "upon a Marsh in Ittchicaw Creek." (see CLOUTER CREEK, WATROO)

ITTIWAN – Alternative spelling for ETIWAN, it was the original name of the COOPER RIVER as well as the early name given to DANIEL ISLAND. A 1676 grant to William Jones was for 210 acres "situated upon an Island commonly called Ittiwan Island." (see CONCISE HISTORY; also ETIWAN, MAWAN)

JAMESTOWN – Town on the South SANTEE RIVER, originally settled by the French HUGUENOTS in the late 1600s. (see CONCISE HISTORY; also ECHAW, FRENCH SANTEE, HELL HOLE SWAMP, JOHN LAWSON)

JASPER, SERGEANT WILLIAM (d. 1779) – Hero at the Battle of Fort Sullivan, June 28, 1776. Recruited from Georgia, Jasper gained fame when a cannonball broke the fort's flagstaff and, despite heavy enemy fire, he leapt over the side of the fort and replaced it. General PETER HORRY later wrote of Jasper's heroism, "he deliberately walked the whole length of the fort, until he came to the colors on the extremity of the left, when he cut off the same from the mast, and called to me for a sponge staff, and with a thick cord tied on the colors and stuck the staff on the rampart in the sand." Ironically, in September 1779, Jasper was killed during the Battle of Savannah as he once more attempted to replace the fallen flag. BATTERY JASPER at FORT MOULTRIE was named in his honor. (see BATTERIES & FORTIFICATIONS, REVOLUTIONARY WAR)

JEREMY CREEK – This tributary of BULL'S BAY at McCLELLANVILLE was named for King Jeremy, a SEWEE chief (*c.* 1701) who lived just south of the SANTEE RIVER. Jeremy Island also retains his name. In 1701, Daniel Macgregor had a warrant for 300 acres "at Waha on ye Southside of Santee river which was formerly ye Plantation of King Jeremy." In 1704, Patrick Stewart had a warrant for 500 acres of lands formerly belonging to "King Jeremy and adjoining Macgregor." (see COLLINS CREEK, WASHASHAW)

JETTIES – These manmade rock barriers forming the main shipping channel into Charleston harbor were begun in 1878 and took 17 years to complete. From SULLIVAN'S ISLAND, the north jetty extends 15,443 feet; the south jetty to Morris Island is 19,104 feet. General Quincy A. Gillmore of the U.S. Army Corps of Engineers designed them, and the foundations were built of raft "mattresses," 50-foot rafts covered with hardwood brush and enough 50- to 100-pound stones (called "one man" stones since they could usually be lifted by one man alone) to eventually sink the raft in place. It took 30 to 60 tons of stone to sink a raft. Gillmore died in 1888, before the jetties were completed. The work was completed by the Charleston engineering firm of Colin McK. Grant and George W. Egan. The final cost for building the jetties was $3,906,869.79. (see CROSSING THE BAR, DRUNKEN DICK'S SHOALS, PILOTS)

JIMMIES – The colloquial and GULLAH name for male BLUE CRABS. The male crab's underbelly is pure white, and the apron does not have the pronounced ridges seen on the females, called SHE-CRABS.

JOGGLING BOARD – This unique lowcountry toy from plantation days consists of an 8-to-10–foot cypress plank that rests on two rocking ends. Children play by jumping, or "joggling," on the center plank. The word comes from the African word *jogal*, which means "to rise." (see GULLAH)

JONES HOTEL – Hotel in MOULTRIEVILLE in the early 1800s. From an advertisement on February 5, 1818, "For Sale. One of the best establishments on Sullivan's Island, that well known and beautiful situation called JONES' ESTABLISHMENT, on Sullivan's Island, with two commodious Buildings for a large BOARDING HOUSE or HOTEL, and one of the best Kitchens on the Island, with a Stable for eight horses and Carriage House. For terms apply to Jehu Jones, 35 Broad Street." Jehu Jones was a free black man who also owned the celebrated Jones Hotel on Broad Street in Charleston during this same period.

JONES SHIPYARD – Shipyard located at HADDRELL'S POINT on SHEM CREEK in the 1860s, operated by F.M. Jones. Jones originally built the steamer *PLANTER* for the plantation trade. Because of her shallow draft and speed, she became a valuable Confederate BLOCKADE RUNNER during the CIVIL WAR.

JONES TAVERN – Also known as the THIRTY-TWO MILE INN, this pre-Revolutionary War inn was on the GEORGETOWN ROAD near TIBWIN and a main stop for travelers. It was a large, typical English-style hostelry, with stables and accommodations for overnight stay. In decrepit condition, the inn was torn down in the 1950s. (see INNS & TAVERNS, STRAIGHT REACH)

JUGNOT & HILLIARD FERRY COMPANY – Later known as the MOUNT PLEASANT FERRY COMPANY, it replaced HIBBEN's FERRY at SHEM CREEK. With Oliver Hilliard, Charles Jugnot purchased and developed the land surrounding ALHAMBRA HALL in 1847, developing the village of HILLIARDSVILLE. The new ferry house and dock were built at the foot of FERRY STREET. The four boats in their fleet were the *COFFEE*, the *Mount Pleasant*, the *JAMES HIBBEN*, and the *Massasoit*. (see CONCISE HISTORY; also CENTER STREET, OLD VILLAGE, THE VILLAGE)

KENSINGTON – This former RICE plantation on the western shore of the Cooper River's EAST BRANCH was a long-standing Ball family landholding. It lies between HYDE PARK and LIMERICK. An advertisement in the November 30, 1818 *Southern Patriot* offered the plantation for sale from the estate of John Ball: "Kensington Plantation, in St. John's Parish on the Eastern Branch of Cooper River, containing 108 acres tide land, 95 acres of which are in complete order for cultivation, 741 acres of highland, cleared and wooded, this is a remarkably well settled Plantation, having thereon a two story double dwelling House, with every other building necessary and convenient." The house was owned by historian DR. JOHN IRVING in the mid-1800s. The home was ransacked and gutted in 1865 by POTTER'S RAIDERS at which time the elderly Dr. Irving and his family were driven from the plantation. Wrote Irving, "what was not useful was smashed in wantonness." The original house, erected in 1745, was destroyed by fire in the 1920s. (see CIVIL WAR, CYPRESS BARONY)

KIAWAH – A coastal CUSABO tribe who lived just south of Charleston. The ASHLEY RIVER was originally called Kiawah. Kiawah Island received its name from this tribe. (see CONCISE HISTORY)

KING STREET – Located in the OLD VILLAGE area of MOUNT PLEASANT, this street was originally part of GREENWICH VILLAGE and, along with Queen Street, was named to honor the English monarchs.

KINNEBEC, THE – The name of a social club on SULLIVAN'S ISLAND in the late 1800s.

LAUREL HILL – This CHRIST CHURCH PARISH plantation opposite PARKER ISLAND and BOONE HALL was first granted to Major John Boone in 1694. The avenue of oaks was planted *c.* 1780. In the mid-1800s, it was the residence of Dr. Peter Porcher Bonneau, a signer of the Ordinance of Secession for Christ Church Parish. It is said that after the Federal occupation of MOUNT PLEASANT in 1865, the wife of COLONEL JAMES BEECHER asked permission to personally set the torch to Laurel Hill. Today, only the columns of the house remain. (see BONNEAU BEACH, GREGORIE, PORCHER)

LAUREL HILL-ST. JAMES SANTEE – On the seaboard just south of McCLELLANVILLE, Laurel Hill has long been a Morrison family landholding. Richard Tillia Morrison (1781–1860) was married to Elizabeth Toomer Legare; their son, Richard (1816–1910) married Elizabeth Ann VENNING, daughter of Robert Venning and Eliza WHILDEN. The Morrison family still retains ownership of Laurel Hill. (see TIBWIN, WAPPETAW MEETING HOUSE)

LAURENS, HENRY (1724–1792) – REVOLUTIONARY WAR patriot and

president of the Continental Congress in 1777. Born in Charleston, Laurens was the son of a prosperous HUGUENOT saddler, John Laurens. After serving as a clerk with James Crokatt in England, Laurens returned to CHARLES TOWN and, with George Austin, established Austin & Laurens, one of the most successful mercantile businesses in the colonies. In the ensuing decades, they made a fortune on trade, particularly slaves and RICE, although Laurens later declared, "I abhor slavery." In 1799, he was appointed a commissioner to Holland, and while aboard the ship taking him to that country, he was captured by the British. He was held in the Tower of London for two years until he was exchanged for General LORD CORNWALLIS. He was married to Eleanor Ball, and of their 12 children, only 4 survived to adulthood. His son, Colonel John Laurens, who had served on General George Washington's staff at Yorktown, was killed in a skirmish with the British near the Combahee River in 1782. Laurens' main plantation was MEPKIN on the COOPER RIVER. (see THE BLESSING, HUGUENOTS, LUMBER, MEPKIN, ORANGES, REVOLUTIONARY WAR, SLAVERY, WEST BRANCH)

LAWSON, JOHN (d. 1711) – This English surveyor and explorer traveled from CHARLES TOWN to Virginia in 1700–1701, a thousand-mile trek which became known as Lawson's Long Trail. His journal of this trip was published in 1709 as *A New Voyage to Carolina* and is the first comprehensive discussion of the Carolina flora and fauna and the Native American tribes. After leaving Charleston, Lawson stopped at the BARRIER ISLANDS from SULLIVAN'S ISLAND to BULL'S ISLAND, describing each. He then journeyed inland, stopping at AWENDAW and the SANTEE RIVER, where he visited the HUGUENOT settlements near JAMESTOWN. Lawson eventually settled at New Bern, North Carolina, where he became surveyor-general. In 1711, Lawson was ambushed by the Tuscarora Indians while on a survey party and was put to death by fire torture, whereby the Indians "stuck him full of fine small splinters of torch wood like hogs bristles and so set them gradually afire." (see AWENDAW, BREACH INLET, BULL'S ISLAND, CAPERS ISLAND, CROAKER, FRENCH SANTEE, OAK, OSPREY)

LAZARETTO – Quarantine station established on SULLIVAN'S ISLAND in the early 1700s as a means to keep infectious DISEASE from entering the colony. It was also called the PEST HOUSE. (see DISEASE, GRACE-CHURCH, PEST HOUSE, SLAVERY, STRANGER'S DISEASE)

LEE, GENERAL CHARLES (1731–1782) – Commander of American forces at Charleston at the beginning of the REVOLUTIONARY WAR. Upon arriving to Charleston in 1776, he became concerned about the unfinished Fort Sullivan, dubbing it a "slaughter pen." Lee wanted to abandon the fort and fight the British from the mainland. He was also worried that no bridge connected the island to the mainland in case it was necessary to retreat. Ultimately, a BRIDGE OF BOATS was built. Although he did not participate directly in the Battle of Fort

Sullivan, he did visit WILLIAM MOULTRIE at the fort during the afternoon of the battle, complimenting the troops by remarking that "their behavior would have done honors to the oldest troops." He complimented Moultrie, saying, "Colonel, you are doing so well here . . . you have no occasion for me, so I will go up to town again." (see BRIDGE OF BOATS, COVE INLET BRIDGE)

LEE'S BRIDGE – Constructed during the REVOLUTIONARY WAR on the insistence of GENERAL CHARLES LEE, the first bridge to cross Cove Inlet.

W.H. LEE – The Army post steamer serving FORT MOULTRIE, *c.* 1900.

LESESNE – Pronounced *La-Sayne*. In 1699, French HUGUENOT émigré Isaac Lesesne and his wife, Frances Netherton Lesesne, were granted land on DANIEL ISLAND. Their land became known as THE GROVE plantation. His sons were Daniel, Thomas, and Isaac Lesesne (d. 1772), the last who served on the Royal Assembly. Isaac Lesesne II and his wife, Elizabeth, had seven children: Sarah, Isaac Walter, Ann, Elizabeth, Daniel, Thomas, and William. The Lesesne family was, for a time, invested with the care of the ferry crossing the COOPER RIVER. Their French heritage helped give rise to its colloquial name, CALAIS FERRY. Their DANIEL ISLAND plantation produced indigo, cattle, cotton, and timber for both the local and export market. They also had a LIME KILN to support BRICKMAKING. (See CALAIS & DOVER FERRY, CLEMENT'S FERRY, COTTON, LUMBER)

LETTERED OLIVE – This long and cylindrical sea shell marked with letter-type hieroglyphics (*Olive sayana*) was named by DR. EDMUND RAVENEL in 1834 in honor of fellow conchologist Thomas Say. The lettered olive is the South Carolina state shell.

LEWISVILLE – For a brief period in the late 1700s, it was the name given to portions of the village at CAINHOY. In 1788, Lewis FOGARTIE began selling narrow lots facing the WANDO RIVER, designing a planned community similar to those used by the French in Louisiana—thus, the name Lewisville, also variously spelled as *Louisville*. (see BRICKMAKING, CAINHOY FERRY, FOGARTIE CREEK, WATCOW)

LEXINGTON PLANTATION – On the upper WANDO RIVER in CHRIST CHURCH PARISH, lying between Wagner Creek and Toomer Creek, also part of WANDO PLANTATION. The tract was part of 1,000 acres granted to Landgrave Edmund Bellinger in 1696. In 1704, it was sold to Alexander Parris, who, in 1712, sold the property to Captain John VANDERHORST, Joseph Vanderhorst, and Thomas Lynch. In 1754, Arnoldus Vanderhorst owned the property. It remained in the Vanderhorst family until 1827, when owner A.S. Willington named the plantation "Lexington." It later was owned by the

Wagner, Waring, and McElroy families and, in the 1930s, by Princess Henrietta Hartford Pignatelli. The plantation grew RICE and COTTON, and there was a substantial BRICKMAKING concern on the property in the 19th century. It is now a portion of Dunes West. (see STARVEGUT HALL, VANDERHORST, WANDO PLANTATION)

LIBERTY HILL – A settlement on RIFLE RANGE ROAD at VENNING Road, one of the many settlements evolving from lands given to newly freed slaves after the CIVIL WAR. (see SLAVERY)

LIGHTHOUSE ISLAND – Island at the north end of BULL'S BAY at CAPE ROMAIN, also called RACCOON KEY. A lighthouse has been on this island since 1847.

LIME KILN – The making of lime (also called quicklime) was an important support industry for the numerous BRICKMAKING concerns. Oyster shells were used to provide the needed calcium carbonate; the shells were obtained both from creeks and from the numerous Indian SHELL MIDDENS that dotted the area. Peter VILLEPONTOUX established a lime kiln on SHEM CREEK in the 1740s. (see CONCISE HISTORY; also BRICKMAKING, DEWEES, LESESNE, SHELL MIDDEN, SHEM CREEK, VILLEPONTOUX)

LIMERICK – Former RICE plantation on the western shore of the Cooper River's EAST BRANCH, just north of KENSINGTON. Originally granted to John Gough, Dominick Arthur, and Michael Mahon (from Limerick, Ireland), it was purchased by Daniel HUGER of FRENCH SANTEE in 1698. It remained a Huger landholding until the 1750s, when it was sold to Elias Ball of KENSINGTON. The rice mill on the plantation was built by JONATHAN LUCAS. In its day, Limerick encompassed some 4,000 acres. During the Federal occupation of Charleston, GENERAL JAMES C. BEECHER and his troops stopped at Limerick and demanded dinner, after which his men then ransacked the house and property. The original house, c. 1700 and built of black cypress, burned in the 1920s. (see GENERAL JAMES C. BEECHER, CIVIL WAR, EAST BRANCH, THE HAGAN, HALIDON HILL, HUGER, POTTER'S RAIDERS)

LOGAN – From Aberdeen, Scotland, Colonel George Logan (d. 1722) came to Carolina in 1690 where he set up business as a merchant. By 1698, he had a resident plantation on THOMAS ISLAND; in 1698, he purchased the 460-acre WANDO PLANTATION. Logan was active politically, served in the assembly, and was public receiver from 1703 to 1707. Logan married twice, and by his first wife, he had three children, George Jr. (1720–1773), Patrick, and Helen. In 1719, he married Martha Daniell, the widow of Robert Daniell. The Logan and Daniell families became further connected when Robert Daniell Jr. married Helen Logan and George Logan Jr. married Robert Daniell's daughter, Martha. (see BARTRAM, CHRIST CHURCH PARISH, HUGER, LEXINGTON, STARVEGUT HALL, WEEHOY)

LONG ISLAND – The original name for ISLE OF PALMS, given for the island's unusual length, approximately 7 miles. (see CONCISE HISTORY, SIR HENRY CLINTON, *THE GOLD BUG*, EDGAR ALLAN POE)

LONG POINT – The point of land on the WANDO RIVER, across from the tip of DANIEL ISLAND. Near here was the early village called BERMUDA TOWN and later, BELVUE-BERMUDA plantation. Long Point Road was originally built in 1703. (see BERMUDA TOWN, EGYPT PLANTATION, PALMETTO GROVE, SNEE FARM, VENNING)

LONGWOOD – This former RICE plantation on the Cooper River's EAST BRANCH was originally known as POMPION HILL Plantation, granted to Peter de St. Julien Malacare in the late 1600s. It was later owned by Benjamin Simons I of MIDDLEBURG; in 1738s, it was the residence of Reverend Thomas Hasell, the first rector of ST. THOMAS PARISH. Successive owners included Captain Thomas Shubrick, Gabriel MANIGAULT, and Nathaniel Heyward. It was named Longwood by owner Alfred HUGER in 1823. (see EAST BRANCH, HUGUENOTS, POMPION HILL, RAVENEL)

LOOKOUT TOWER ON SULLIVAN'S ISLAND – In 1702, a lookout tower was ordered for Sullivan's Island, to be built with "Brick Round Twenty five foot Diamitir at Bottome and Twelve feete, Diamiter at Topp, with Two flores and that the foundation to be . . . secured with Pyles." This tower acted as both a watchtower to sight incoming ships and as a recognizable landmark for mariners. The harbor PILOTS used this lookout as their headquarters. James Bassford was the first in charge of the watch at this tower, followed by Captain John Cock Sr. in 1707. In 1713, a new tower was ordered erected, since the previous one had been "overthrown and carried by the late hurricane." Lookout towers and a Lighthouse were on Sullivan's Island throughout its history. (see COASTAL WATCH, COPPER BUOYS, CROSSING THE BAR, PILOTS, SULLIVAN'S ISLAND LIGHT)

LORDS PROPRIETORS – Following the restoration of Charles II to the throne of England in 1660, the king repaid those men who had helped him regain the throne by giving them a generous grant of land in the new world called CAROLINA. These supporters became known as the Lords Proprietors. They were the Earl of Clarendon, Duke of ALBEMARLE, Lord Craven, Lord John BERKELEY, LORD ANTHONY ASHLEY COOPER, Sir George Carteret, Sir William Berkeley, and Sir John COLLETON. (see CONCISE HISTORY; also BARONY, FUNDAMENTAL CONSTITUTIONS)

LUCAS (PINCKNEY), ELIZA (1722–1792) – Eliza Lucas was the daughter of Colonel George Lucas, a former governor of Antigua. Her successful experiments with the processing of INDIGO in 1740–41 helped make this crop an important export for Carolina plantations. Married to Governor Charles PINCKNEY, she was the mother of Charles Cotesworth Pinckney and her daughter, Harriott, was married to Daniel Horry of HAMPTON PLANTATION. It was here that she entertained President George Washington during his Southern Tour in 1781. Washington thought so much of Mrs. Pinckney that upon her death in Philadelphia in 1792, he was a pallbearer at her funeral. (see INDIGO, HAMPTON PLANTATION)

LUCAS, JONATHAN (1754–1821) – Born in Cumberland, England, Lucas was an educated millwright when he accidentally arrived on the Carolina coast near the SANTEE RIVER in 1787, the ship on which he was aboard was blown ashore by a storm. While staying at Peachtree Plantation, he saw the laborious way RICE was cleaned and prepared for market by hand. He invented a water-driven rice milling operation and soon became wealthy building mills for area plantations. On what became known as MILL ISLAND, Lucas constructed a wind-powered lumber and saw mill. In 1795, he built the first water-driven, combined rice and saw mill in the Charleston area on SHEM CREEK. The adjoining lands became known as Lucasville, with Lucas Street and MILL STREET later named for this brilliant inventor and his mill. Lucas was married to Mary Cook, and their son, Jonathan Lucas II (1775–1832), married Lydia Simons, the daughter of Benjamin Simons III of MIDDLEBURG Plantation. (see HOG ISLAND, HYDE PARK, LIMERICK, MIDDLEBURG, MILL ISLAND, SHEM CREEK, VENNING, WASHO)

LUMBER – A profitable asset for plantations in CHRIST CHURCH PARISH and ST. THOMAS PARISH, lumber products were provided to both the Charleston market and area shipbuilders. In 1763, HENRY LAURENS ordered a large quantity of lumber from Stephen Miller at CAINHOY, including 30 beams, 25,000 shingles, and more than 5,000 feet of plank, "free from Sap and knots." Laurens also purchased lumber from Isaac and Daniel LESESNE. "I must have none but the very best board," he wrote. "Of as great lengths as can be procur'd and properly saw'd for the purpose of sheathing the Bottoms of Ships." When Richard Beresford Jr. advertised the sale of 12 properties (almost 7,000 acres) in the July 4–11, 1760 *Gazette*, he stated that, among other things, the plantations could "supply ship carpenters with spars and white oak, and the block makers and wheelrights with ash." (see CONCISE HISTORY; also BONNEAU FERRY, BUCKET FACTORY, CHILDSBURY, DANIEL ISLAND, GROVE PLANTATION, HENRY LAURENS, LESESNE, LEXINGTON, MILL ISLAND, WANDO PLANTATION)

LYNCH'S GROVE – This plantation in CHRIST CHURCH PARISH off MATHIS FERRY Road in the area called WAKENDAW was one of several owned by Thomas Lynch (1675–1738) and, later, his son, Thomas (1726–1776), and grandson, Thomas Lynch Jr. (1749-1779), a signer of the Declaration of

Independence. Thomas Lynch Jr. was married to Elizabeth Shubrick and their home plantation was Peachtree Plantation on the South SANTEE RIVER at WASHO. The first Thomas Lynch emigrated from Ireland in the 1670s. His grants were primarily choice tidal marshes where he erected RICE plantations, such as HOPSEWEE on the South Santee River. (see CONCISE HISTORY; also COINBOW CREEK, HOPSEWEE, LEXINGTON PLANTATION, JONATHAN LUCAS, SALT HOPE/SALT PONDS, REVOLUTIONARY WAR, WATTESAW)

MAGWOOD – This family long affiliated with SHEM CREEK and BULL'S ISLAND began in South Carolina with Irishman Simon Magwood (1763–1836). Captain Robert Holman Magwood (1878–1956) purchased the Mount Pleasant Boat Building Company on Shem Creek in 1895, and his boats *Susie Magwood* and *Josephine* were kept there, as was his COOTER pen, a turtle crawl where he raised diamondback terrapins for export to Northern restaurants. In the 1930s, Captain William C. Magwood introduced the first powered shrimp trawler on the creek, the *Skipper*. The Magwood family continues to dock their shrimpboats on Shem Creek. (see COOTER, SHEM CREEK)

MANHATTAN, THE – A social club on SULLIVAN'S ISLAND in the late 1890s.

MANIGAULT – French HUGUENOT émigré Pierre Manigault (pronounced *Man-i-go*) settled at FRENCH SANTEE in the 1690s, marking the beginning of one of the most prominent families in Carolina. Gabriel Manigault (1704–1791) became the wealthiest merchant and private banker in the province. He so abhorred the slave trade that he refused to lend money to those involved in the business, although he did, himself, own 289 slaves that worked his RICE plantations. The SEWEE BARONY plantations at AWENDAW were among the many Manigault holdings, remaining in that family until the late 1800s. His son was Peter Manigault (1731–1773). Descendants of Manigault family slaves are known for their artistry and skill at making SWEETGRASS BASKETS, some of which are in the permanent collection of the Smithsonian Institute. (see FRENCH SANTEE, LONGWOOD, SALT HOPE/SALT PONDS, SEWEE BARONY, SILK HOPE, SLAVERY)

MARION, GENERAL FRANCIS (1732–1795) – Born near GEORGETOWN, Marion was the son of French HUGUENOT émigré Gabriel Marion. This REVOLUTIONARY WAR hero was dubbed "The Swamp Fox" by British General Sir Banestre Tarleton after Marion eluded him by slipping into a nearby swamp. Successfully fighting guerrilla warfare against the British, Marion and his brigade of partisan rangers (which varied from 20 to 100 men, depending on circumstances) became famous for their daring forays against the enemy. Marion's last order to fight came on November 16, 1782, when he was given orders by General Nathaniel Greene to go after British foragers at HOBCAW. The war all but over, he refused, stating that enough blood had been shed in the cause of freedom, and he would not spill another drop of it. In 1785, at age 54, he married his cousin Mary Videau. He served in the assembly and was a member of the 1790 South Carolina constitutional convention. He died at his plantation, Pond Bluff, in 1795. (see HELL HOLE SWAMP, HUGUENOTS, REVOLUTIONARY WAR, WADBOO)

MAROON – An early term of an outdoor party, hunting, or fishing expedition. Miss Harriott PINCKNEY told of a the "belles and beaus" attending a maroon held on SULLIVAN'S ISLAND in 1801, writing, "Our first maroon passed off very well . . . we had about as many beaus as belles."

MARSHALL RESERVATION – The northernmost point on SULLIVAN'S ISLAND overlooking BREACH INLET. This area's military history started with a battery erected here in 1776 by Colonel William Thompson to halt the British attempting to cross from LONG ISLAND (now ISLE OF PALMS). During the CIVIL WAR, BATTERY MARSHALL was erected by Confederate forces, named to honor Colonel J. Foster Marshall, CSA, who was killed in Virginia. During World War II, large hill-shaped batteries were erected near this same site and, although their official military name was Construction 520, they became known as Fort Marshall, presumably from the previous Confederate battery. Begun in May 1943, the construction of these batteries was complete by year's end. The two 12-inch guns were 420 feet apart, sited to allow each a 145-degree field of fire, with a range of 29,300 yards. These installations now have been remodeled into private homes. During World War II, the entire area of Marshall Reservation was a busy military installation with barracks and other support buildings for FORT MOULTRIE. (see BATTERIES & FORTIFICATIONS, C.S.S. *HUNLEY*)

MASTODON BONES – In 1859, while working on his plantation, Cedar Grove, which was on the western shore of SHEM CREEK (now Cooper Estates), Dr. Louis F. Klipstein discovered fragments of mastodon bones while ditching and excavating a pond. Portions of the tusk measuring more than 6 feet were also found. Characterized by elongated noses and tusks (like elephants), the *mastodon americanus* was a mammal of the Pleistocene period, the last ice age. The mastodon had a shoulder height of 10 feet or more. (see CONCISE HISTORY)

MATHEWS FERRY – In 1700, Captain Anthony Mathews (1661–1735) began the first ferry service linking HOBCAW to CHARLES TOWN, which came to be known as Mathew's Ferry. Shortly afterwards, an act was passed to build "one common road, of 16 feet wide" to link the ferry with the GEORGETOWN ROAD. Over time, this road became known as MATHIS FERRY Road, a shortened, GULLAH-influenced version of Mathew's Ferry. Originally from London, Captain Mathews was a merchant in Charles Town. His son was Anthony Mathews Jr. (1697–1756). Captain Mathews is buried in the cemetery at the Circular Congregational Church in Charleston. (see CONCISE HISTORY; also HOBCAW POINT, TIBWIN)

MATHIS FERRY Road – An adaptation of MATHEWS FERRY.

MAWAN – A Native American name attributed to DANIEL ISLAND, or perhaps THOMAS ISLAND. In 1706, Christopher Smyth's will leaves his granddaughter, Mary Beresford, land on an "island commonly called Mawan, since Thomas' or Col. Daniell's Island." The more familiar Native American name for Daniel Island was ITTIWAN.

McCANTS DRIVE – This street in Mount Pleasant's OLD VILLAGE becomes RIFLE RANGE ROAD after it crosses Ben Sawyer Boulevard. It was named for Thomas Gadsden McCants, mayor of Mount Pleasant from 1928 to 1933.

McCLELLANVILLE – Located on JEREMY CREEK overlooking BULL'S BAY, this small village is approximately 28 miles north of MOUNT PLEASANT. It was founded in the 1820s as a summer RESORT for SANTEE RIVER planters. The village takes its name from Scotsman Archibald McClellan, who settled in this section in 1771. For most of the past century, the village economy has been centered around the commercial shrimping, oystering, and crabbing industry. Surrounding truck farms also provide vegetables to both a local and national market. Longstanding McClellanville families include the Morrison, Leland, DuPré, PINCKNEY, Doar, and Graham families, among others. (see BULL'S BAY, CHAPEL OF EASE, COUNTRY FEVER, JEREMY CREEK, LAUREL HILL, RESORTS, ST. JAMES SANTEE, TIBWIN, THE VILLAGE, WAPPETAW)

McCORMICK, H.L.P. – Henry Laurens Pinckney McCormick (1831–1894) was intendant of MOUNT PLEASANT from 1874 to 1876. He was also owner of the MOUNT PLEASANT FERRY COMPANY during this same period. Buried at the CONFEDERATE CEMETERY in Mount Pleasant, his marker reads, "Faithful, Fearless, Just and Generous."

McINTIRE'S BOARDING HOUSE – A popular summer retreat on SULLIVAN'S ISLAND at MOULTRIEVILLE in the 1830s.

MEPKIN – This bluff and creek on the eastern shore of the Cooper River's WEST BRANCH near WADBOO takes its name from an Indian word, perhaps "Makkean" or "Mebken," meaning unknown. Mepkin was the country seat of HENRY LAURENS, purchased from John COLLETON in 1762. The 7,000-acre RICE plantation remained in the Laurens family until the early 1900s. In 1936, Mepkin was purchased by wealthy publisher Henry Luce and his wife, Claire Booth Luce. They bequeathed the property to Trappist monks of the Cistercian Order in the 1960s, and today the plantation is known as Mepkin Abbey. The now 3,200-

acre property serves as a spiritual retreat with portions of the plantation open to the public. (see COLLETON, HENRY LAURENS, LUMBER, ORANGES, WEST BRANCH)

MIDDLEBURG – Former RICE plantation on the eastern shore of the Cooper River's EAST BRANCH, just south of POMPION HILL, granted to French HUGUENOT émigré Benjamin Simons I (1672–1717) in the 1690s. The name comes from Middleburg in the Netherlands, where Simons took refuge after leaving France. The original house, erected *c.* 1697, still stands and is considered the oldest frame dwelling in South Carolina. Other outbuildings include the ruins of the former rice mill and steam engine built by JONATHAN LUCAS. It is privately owned and on the National Historic Register. (see EAST BRANCH, THE GROVE, HALIDON HILL, WILLIAM HORT, LONGWOOD, JONATHAN LUCAS)

MILL ISLAND – An island at CAPE ROMAIN near RACCOON KEY. The island takes its name from the wind-powered lumber and saw mill built here by JONATHAN LUCAS. (see BULL'S BAY)

MILL STREET – In MOUNT PLEASANT on the east side of SHEM CREEK, this street was named for the water-driven rice mill, *c.* 1795, built by JONATHAN LUCAS. (see OLD VILLAGE)

MILTON'S FERRY – The ferry operation at HOBCAW POINT in the 1830s.

MOCKINGBIRD – This indigenous songbird (*Mimus polyglottos*) is legendary for its ability to "mock" other birds. In 1682, Thomas Ashe wrote that this bird "wantonly imitates the various Notes and Sounds of such Birds and Beasts which it hears, wherefore, by way of illusion, it is called the Mocking Bird." Naturalist MARK CATESBY noted that the Native Americans called the mockingbird "Cencontlatollya" or "four hundred tongues." Both males and females help build and protect their nests.

MOLASSES CREEK – A small tidal tributary of the WANDO RIVER at HOBCAW POINT. The creek's first mention was in 1701 when BENJAMIN QUELCH agreed to sell to Richard Dearsley, "all that plantation containing 330 acres of land bounding on land of David Maybanck, west on Wando river, North on Wakendaw Creek and South on creek called Molasses Creek." The source of the name is not known; perhaps, it was for the dark color of the water against its banks of PLOUGH MUD.

MONCKS CORNER – Town and county seat of BERKELEY COUNTY, named for Thomas Monck, who was the landowner in the area on which the town was built, *c.* 1735.

MONROE, PRESIDENT JAMES (1758–1831) – In April 1819, President Monroe visited Charleston, and upon his arrival, he was rowed to Charleston in an elegant barge, leaving from GORDON & SPRINGS FERRY at HOBCAW with members of the Marine Society at the oars. During his stay, he took the steamer *Charleston* to SULLIVAN'S ISLAND, where he reviewed the troops at FORT MOULTRIE and dined with Jacob Bond I'on. (see HOBCAW FERRY, I'ON)

MOONSHINE – During Prohibition, the hinterlands of HELL HOLE SWAMP and along the SANTEE RIVER were ideal for the manufacture of illegal whiskey. A report in the August 4, 1928 *News & Courier* noted that "The discovery of two caves on the Santee River . . . has led to the destruction of 1,600 gallons of red whisky." On September 8, 1928, the *Courier* reported that 42 gallons of whisky "hot from the still" were seized as it was being transported from BERKELEY COUNTY. Despite being illegal, these whisky-making operations were largely overlooked by authorities. (see BOOTLEGGING, HELL HOLE SWAMP)

MORELAND – Plantation on the COOPER RIVER's eastern bank just above DANIEL ISLAND, also known as THE BRICKYARD. An advertisement in the November 22, 1760 *Gazette* noted: "Bricks to be Sold, in any Quantity from 6,000 to several hundred thousand, by JOHN MOORE of St. Thomas Parish. Orders left at Messrs. Neufvilles will be forwarded." The original name "Moreland" most likely originated from original owner John Moore, who died in 1732. (see BRICKMAKING, THE BRICKYARD)

MORRIS ISLAND LIGHTHOUSE – The first Morris Island light was erected in 1752 to replace the lighthouse on SULLIVAN'S ISLAND that had been destroyed by a storm. The present Morris Island lighthouse was built in 1876 and is 161 feet tall. Severe erosion has consumed most of Morris Island, and the lighthouse now stands in Lighthouse Inlet off the north end of Folly Island. The Morris Island Light remained active until 1962, when the SULLIVAN'S ISLAND lighthouse was erected. It now serves only as a day mark. (see CROSSING THE BAR)

MOTTE – John Abraham Motte (original French name, de la Motte) was a French HUGUENOT refugee who came to CHARLES TOWN in 1700, first by way of Dublin, then Antigua. While in Antigua, he contracted with John Perrie to become the manager of Perrie's affairs in Carolina. In 1704, he purchased for Perrie a plantation on the seacoast mainland of MOUNT PLEASANT, which they named YOUGHALL. His son, Jacob Motte (1700–1770), became one of the colony's wealthiest and most influential men and was in partnership with John Lauren's, the father of HENRY LAURENS. Motte served as a member of the assembly and was public treasurer of CAROLINA for almost 30 years. In 1749, Jacob Motte purchased the tract called MOUNT PLEASANT PLANTATION, from which the town was eventually named. (see CONCISE HISTORY; also GRAY BAY, GRAY'S FERRY, HIBBEN, OAKLAND PLANTATION, VILLEPONTOUX)

MOULTRIE, GENERAL WILLIAM (1731–1805) – The son of Dr. John Moultrie (1702–1771) and his wife, Lucretia Cooper. Even before the REVOLUTIONARY WAR, Moultrie had distinguished himself as a leader in the Cherokee Wars, c. 1761. Appointed colonel of the 2nd Colonial Regiment, in 1776, he was given the task of building fortifications in the Charleston area, including an order to build Fort Sullivan on Sullivan's Island, which he erected with materials close at hand, particularly PALMETTO logs. When the British fleet opened fire on the fort, Moultrie so astutely used his limited ammunition that the overconfident British fleet assumed the half-finished fort was no real threat and sailed in closer. Within easy range, the Americans released a barrage that left the British fleet in ruins. To honor Moultrie's brilliance during this battle, he was promoted to the rank of brigadier general and Fort Sullivan was renamed FORT MOULTRIE. The RESORT community at the lower end of SULLIVAN'S ISLAND was also named MOULTRIEVILLE in his honor. Moultrie later served twice as governor of South Carolina. He is buried at the fort, at a site overlooking THE COVE. (see CONCISE HISTORY; also BATTERIES & FORTIFICATIONS, BRIDGE OF BOATS, CAINHOY MEETING HOUSE, *CHEROKEE* and *TAMAR*, CLINTON, DORRELL, FRANCIS MARION, PETER HORRY, GENERAL CHARLES LEE, LEE'S BRIDGE, PINCKNEY, REVOLUTIONARY WAR)

MOULTRIE HOUSE – This grand hotel on SULLIVAN'S ISLAND at MOULTRIEVILLE opened July 8, 1850, with accommodations for 200 people. Located just to the west of FORT MOULTRIE, it offered a spectacular view of both harbor and ocean. The Moultrie House became one of the most popular resorts on the Eastern Seaboard, famous for fine foods and "no deficiency of amusements," including four billiard tables, three bowling saloons, horses for riding, boats for fishing and "none but the choicest liquors." The hotel was huge; 256 feet long and 40 feet wide, with an elegant 110-foot-long ballroom. To the rear of the building were the kitchens and a large bath for the ladies, supplied with water from a windmill. During the first bombardment of FORT SUMTER, Union officer ABNER DOUBLEDAY fired a shell directly at the top story of the hotel, causing serious damage. Later, when asked why he had fired at a civilian target, Doubleday explained that "the landlord had given me a wretched room there one night, and this being the only opportunity that had occurred to get even with him, I was unable to resist it."

MOULTRIEVILLE – The name given to the early RESORT settlement at the southern tip of SULLIVAN'S ISLAND. When the township incorporated in 1819, the area had 200 summer houses in addition to FORT MOULTRIE. Beginning in the late 1700s, Charlestonians and east of the Cooper planters began "resorting" to Moultrieville each summer to avoid the COUNTRY FEVER and other diseases. Private homes, hotels, and boarding houses were filled during the summer months, with ferry boats making daily trips between Charleston and the island. By 1850, Moultrieville was one of the most popular resorts on the east coast, with the expansive MOULTRIE HOUSE at its center. During the CIVIL WAR, most of the houses on the island were abandoned or destroyed. In the 1870s, Moultrieville began to recover and, at the turn of the century, much of Moultrieville held support buildings and residences for officers and men at Fort Moultrie. The end of the island below the fort, however, remained primarily residential. (see CONCISE HISTORY; also DR. LOUIS AGASSIZ, ATLANTICVILLE, CHENEY'S BOARDING HOUSE, CIVIL WAR, GRACE-CHURCH, JONES HOTEL, McINTIRE'S BOARDING HOUSE, MOULTRIE HOUSE, SEASIDE LABORATORY, STATIONS, WILKIE'S BOARDING HOUSE, POINT HOUSE)

MOUNT EDGECOMBE – Name given in 1730 to his plantation on HOG ISLAND (now PATRIOT'S POINT) by Captain John Gascoigne, perhaps for a family estate in England.

MOUNT PLEASANT ACADEMY – This school (now on CENTER STREET) was originally established in the OLD VILLAGE in 1809, with the Reverend Aaron W. Leland, headmaster.

MOUNT PLEASANT FERRY COMPANY – Also known as the Mount Pleasant & Sullivan's Island Ferry Company. This ferry linking Charleston, Mount Pleasant, and Sullivan's Island was established by JUGNOT & HILLIARD, *c.* 1847. (see ALHAMBRA HALL, HILLIARDSVILLE, H.L.P. McCORMICK, *POCOSIN*, *SAPPHO*)

MOUNT PLEASANT HOTEL – From an advertisement in the April 10, 1854 *Courier*: "Mount Pleasant Hotel, H. KAMLAH, Proprietor – This House is now open for public reception, and the proprietor has spared no expense to make his house one of the finest in the Southern country. All he asks is a fair trial and an impartial verdict." Boarding and lodging for one day was $2.00 or $10.00 per week. Dinner was 75 cents. The hotel burned to the ground on January 24, 1861.

MOUNT PLEASANT PLANTATION – Name of Jacob MOTTE's plantation from which the town eventually received its name. The main plantation house became known as the HIBBEN HOUSE for subsequent owner James HIBBEN. It has been stated that the name Mount Pleasant was given for the area's moderately high bluff in an otherwise flat geography. The name was, however, one of the most popular estate names of the 18th century in both England and America, and there were three other Mount Pleasant plantations in the lowcountry at this same time. (see CONCISE HISTORY; also LORD CHARLES CORNWALLIS, GRAY BAY, GRAY'S FERRY, HIBBEN, HOG ISLAND HILL)

MOUNT PLEASANT PRESBYTERIAN CHURCH – In OLD VILLAGE at 302 Hibben Street, this is the oldest church in Mount Pleasant, established in 1827 by the congregation at Wappetaw to serve those who had built summer residences along the harbor front. the first church building was erected at 226 Bennett Street. The present white clapboard edifice was erected in the 1870s. During the CIVIL WAR the church was as a Confederate hospital and the original pews and pulpit were removed. Notches for the beds in the balcony are still visible today. (see RESORTS, WAPPETAW MEETING HOUSE)

MUGGRIDGE'S BOARDING HOUSE – Mrs. Muggridge's Boarding House was on SULLIVAN'S ISLAND at MOULTRIEVILLE in the 1830s.

MYERS, COLONEL – From an advertisement in the April 10, 1854 *Courier*: "EXCURSION AROUND THE HARBOR: The Steamer COL. MYERS will make an excursion around The Harbor, touching at Sullivan's Island, Tomorrow, leaving Atlantic Wharf at 4 o'clock P.M. and return at sunset. Fare 25 cents for the Trip. A Band of Music will be on board."

MYRTLE – The hardy, aromatic sweet myrtle, or wax myrtle (*Myrica cerifera*), also known as bayberry. MARK CATESBY called it the "Narrow-leaved Candleberry Tree" for the berries it produces that were once used to make candles. Catesby wrote, "In November and December, at which time the berries are mature, a man with his family will remove from his home to some island or sandbanks near the sea, where these trees most abound, taking with him kettles to boil the berries in . . . they boil them until the oil floats, which is skimmed off into another vessel. This is repeated until there remains no more oil. This, when cold, hardens to the consistency of wax, and is of a dirty green color. They then boil it again, and clarify it in grass kettles; which gives it a transparent greenness." Also esteemed for its medicinal properties, the boiled root bark produced an astringent and stimulant used as both a headache remedy and a curative for scrofula, jaundice, diarrhea, and dysentery. A tea made from the leaves was thought to relieve an aching back, "clean out the kidneys," and overcome chills. (see CANDLEBERRY TREE, MARK CATESBY)

MYRTLES, THE – On SULLIVAN'S ISLAND, the name formerly given to an area of thickets and bushes along the back beach and towards the northern end the island, so called for the proliferation of wax myrtle trees. In 1843, Frederick Adolphus PORCHER wrote, "Just behind our house were the first of those hills which I suppose the action of the wind had raised on the Island, which continued to rise higher and higher from this point to the northeast extremity of the Island. Over these hills are what are called the Myrtles, then we come to the back beach by which the distance to the Cove is reduced more than a third, and the road excellent." In *THE GOLD BUG*, EDGAR ALLAN POE wrote, "the whole island, with the exception of this western point, and a line of hard white beach on the seacoast, is covered with a dense undergrowth of the sweet myrtle, so much prized by the horticulturists of England." (see I'ON AVENUE, MOULTRIEVILLE)

MYRTLE GROVE – This plantation on the seacoast mainland of CHRIST CHURCH PARISH was the main residence of the VENNING family in earlier centuries. (see VENNING)

NAKED LADY LILY – This white swamp Atamasco lily earned its nickname from the fact that it grows on one slender, leafless stalk offering a simple white bloom. Blooming in spring, they are found throughout the forests and swamps of the coastal regions. (see CAROLINA BAYS)

NELLIEFIELD CREEK – This creek on the CAINHOY peninsula perhaps is a GULLAH adaptation of the French HUGUENOT name *Neufville*. (see MORELAND)

NEW BRIGHTON HOTEL – A large hotel in ATLANTICVILLE on SULLIVAN'S ISLAND in the late 1800s. The centerpiece of Atlanticville's Ocean Park, this was a grand beachfront hotel fronted by a large pavilion on the beach, a boardwalk, and bathhouses jutting into the surf. A July 4, 1885 *Courier* article announced Independence Day festivities on the island: "The New Brighton Hotel is prepared to accommodate the crowd and a special dinner will be served in honor of the occasion. The well known Boston band, which is engaged for the season, will give three open air concerts during the day, and those who prefer will be served with refreshments on the verandah of the hotel." Weekend dances called "hops" were also held on the verandah for Charlestonians who took the ferry to Mount Pleasant and then the trolley over to the island for the day. The New Brighton was destroyed by fire and later replaced by the ATLANTIC BEACH HOTEL. (see CHARLESTON & SEASHORE RAILROAD COMPANY, ISLE OF PALMS)

NICARAGUAN VICTORY – Merchant ship that rammed into the COOPER RIVER BRIDGE (the Grace Memorial Bridge) on February 24, 1946, bringing down a portion of the WANDO RIVER span. The accident occurred during a sudden storm that caused the ship to slip anchor. This tragedy resulted in the loss of a family of five whose car was on the bridge at the time. It took over six months to repair the bridge, during which time the ferry service was reestablished to link MOUNT PLEASANT and Charleston.

NORTH POINT – Early name of the point of land in MOUNT PLEASANT by the OLD BRIDGE. At times, this was also called BARKSDALE'S POINT and OLDWANUS POINT. (see OLD VILLAGE)

NO-SEE-UM – Colloquial term (possibly a GULLAH derivation) for the small, biting insects known as gnats. They are so tiny that you "no-see-um."

OAK – Explorer JOHN LAWSON wrote that of the oak's durability, "A Nail once driven therein, 'tis next to an Impossibility to draw it out." He also noted the many uses of the acorn by the coastal Indians, stating that "the Indians draw an Oil from them, as sweet as that from the Olive." Oak was esteemed by area shipbuilders. An advertisement in the *Gazette* of January 26, 1760, announced, "This is to acquaint all masters of vessels, shiprights, &c., that they may be supplied with LIVE-OAK TIMBER, such as standards, breast-hooks, transoms, stems, knees &c, for . . . any person wanting a frame for a schooner or boat." Oak was also more impervious to destructive marine borers and did not rot in salt water like other less durable woods. (see LUMBER)

OAKLAND PLANTATION – Originally called YOUGHALL, this plantation began as a 1,300-acre tract granted to George Dearsley in 1696. Portions were later sold to Thomas Hamlin and William Capers. In 1704, the remaining 982 acres were sold to Abraham MOTTE, acting as agent for the Perrie family from Antigua. The plantation came into the PORCHER and GREGORIE families in 1859. The house was then owned by Philip Edward PORCHER. The plantation house is one of the few in CHRIST CHURCH PARISH still standing. It is said that after Charleston fell into Union hands in 1865, the house and outbuildings were about to be put to the torch when the former slaves interceded. (see GENERAL JAMES CHAPLIN BEECHER, CIVIL WAR, CONFEDERATE LINES, GREGORIE, YOUGHALL)

OCEAN GROVE CEMETERY – The name of the cemetery in Mount Pleasant's OLD VILLAGE bordered by McCANTS DRIVE and SIMMONS STREET. It is also called St. Paul's Cemetery. The pathway running through the center of the cemetery is colloquially known as Hallelujah Lane.

OFFICER'S ROW – A row of nearly identical, two-story houses built *c.* 1903 for FORT MOULTRIE officers and their families on I'ON AVENUE between Stations 17 and 18 on SULLIVAN'S ISLAND. At each end of this row are larger houses—the fort commander's house at Station 17 and the Bachelor Officers' Quarters at Station 18 (now Sandpiper apartments). When first built, these houses commanded a view of the ocean, and a small golf course was erected between the dunes and the houses. They are now private homes.

O'HEAR'S POINT – The point of land at the sharp bend in the WANDO RIVER just above CAINHOY. Planter and brickmaker John O'Hear also owned WANDO PLANTATION in CHRIST CHURCH PARISH. O'Hear's Point had a BRICKYARD, producing approximately 580,000 bricks a year. In the 1850s, O'Hear operated the CAINHOY FERRY. In more recent years, the point has been owned by the Mason Smith family and known as "Riverbend." (see BRICKMAKING, CAINHOY FERRY, LEXINGTON)

OLD BRIDGE – Now maintained by the town of MOUNT PLEASANT as a recreational area for fishing, shrimping, and crabbing, the old COVE INLET

BRIDGE was once the trolley bridge joining SULLIVAN'S ISLAND and MOUNT PLEASANT. Various bridges were built here, beginning with a BRIDGE OF BOATS during the REVOLUTIONARY WAR. The bridge was dismantled when the causeway was built to Sullivan's Island in 1935. (see CHARLESTON & SEASHORE RAILROAD COMPANY, COVE INLET BRIDGE, ISLE OF PALMS, LEE'S BRIDGE, REVOLUTIONARY WAR)

OLD FORT, OLD PALMETTO FORT – A small marsh island just off the MOUNT PLEASANT mainland on HAMLIN SOUND, this island has a relatively high bluff of oyster shells, so it may have originally been a Sewee SHELL MIDDEN. This is purported to be one of the places the French and Spanish attacked in 1706. (see FRENCH-SPANISH INVASION)

OLD VILLAGE – The colloquial name given to the original town of MOUNT PLEASANT, the area generally between SHEM CREEK and the OLD BRIDGE, with ROYALL AVENUE forming its northern boundary. Its main thoroughfare is PITT STREET and until the 1970s, this street was the center of the town's business and social activities, with grocery store, post office, hardware store, pharmacy, and doctors' offices. Many of the homes date to the 19th century. The area is on the National Historic Register. (see ALHAMBRA HALL, GREENWICH VILLAGE, HILLIARDSVILLE, OLD BRIDGE, PATJEN'S POST OFFICE)

OLDWANUS POINT – The exact meaning is not known, but the name was probably that given by the Indians for the point of land in MOUNT PLEASANT by the OLD BRIDGE, also at times called Old Woman's Point, BARKSDALE'S POINT, and NORTH POINT.

ONESICAU – SEWEE name for BULL'S ISLAND. It is also spelled ANISECAU. In 1698, Samuel Hartley sold Thomas Cary 1,580 acres on the island "known by ye name of One-si-cau." (see BARRIER ISLANDS, BULL'S ISLAND, HUNTING ISLANDS)

OPOSSUM – The name for this nocturnal mammal comes from the Virginia Indian word *apasum*, meaning "white beast." Indigenous to lowcountry swamps, forests, and neighborhoods, these animals pretend to be dead if caught, thus the term "playing possum."

ORANGE QUARTER – Early name for the area on the Cooper River's EAST BRANCH settled by French HUGUENOT families in the late 1600s. The name may have been given to honor William Prince of Orange (William I of England), who owned the principality of Orange near Avignon, France. It was here that the French church of ST. DENIS was erected. In 1698/9, the population of French settlers in the Orange Quarter was given as 101. After 1715, the area became to be known as the FRENCH QUARTER. (see EAST BRANCH, FRENCH PROTESTANTS, HUGUENOTS, ST. DENIS)

ORANGES – A sweet orange was a delicacy in the 18th century, and orange groves were attempted with success until a series of unusually severe winters in the 1740s and 1750s. Orange groves were on SHUTE'S FOLLY Island and HOG ISLAND, as well as on many of the plantations. HENRY LAURENS of MEPKIN was a cultivator of oranges; also DR. SAMUEL CARNE.

OSCEOLA (1804–1838) – Seminole chief brought to FORT MOULTRIE as a prisoner in 1838. Federal Indian agents were directed to take Seminole lands and forcibly move the tribe to Oklahoma. One agent also captured Osceola's wife (a free black woman) and sold her into slavery. Osceola retaliated by killing the agent responsible. He then began a series of raids from his Everglades hideaway against the white villages and forts, precipitating the second War of the Seminoles. When Osceola agreed to meet with General Thomas Jesup to discuss a treaty, he was instead seized, taken first to prison in St. Augustine, and then moved to Fort Moultrie, where he became ill and died. Jesup's actions became a national embarrassment. Osceola was buried with full military honors at the entrance to the fort.

OSPREY – Also called "sea eagles" or "fish hawks," the osprey (*Pandion haliaetus*) has a wingspan of 5–7 feet and is marked with a white head, brown back, and white underbelly. Their feet have special pads that allow them to hold fish (a wet and slippery prey) in place. Explorer JOHN LAWSON called the osprey the "Eagle's Jackal," writing that "he builds his Nest as Eagles do; that is, in a dead Cypress tree, either standing in, or hard by, the Water." Osprey nests are seen throughout the coastal region, often built on power poles.

O'SULLIVAN, CAPTAIN FLORENCE – One of the original colonists to arrive in 1670 on the ship *CAROLINA*, O'Sullivan was granted 2,340 acres of land in what is now the OLD VILLAGE of MOUNT PLEASANT, just south of SHEM CREEK. Although SULLIVAN'S ISLAND was named after him, it is unclear if he actually owned the island. In 1674, he was given charge of the watch on the island and a "great Gunn to be fired on the approach of any ship or ships." O'Sullivan had a sterling record as a military man but, as the colony's first surveyor-general, he was inept and lost that position within one year. He was also known for being a contentious, difficult man, and early documents carry repeated complaints about his behavior. Still, O'Sullivan remained an important man in the colony and was commissioner of public accounts until his death, *c.* 1683.

OYSTER – The common oyster (*Crassostrea virginica*) is abundantly found in lowcountry creeks and marshes. These irregularly shaped, razor sharp bivalves live in clusters in beds of PLOUGH MUD and are harvested in winter months. The oyster has played a far wider role in lowcountry history than that of a mere foodstuff. The coastal Indians constructed their SHELL RINGS from oyster and other shells. As the building material called TABBY, crushed oyster shell was used as an important construction material in colonial times. Likewise, it was used in the construction of early roads. It was the basic material from which the LIME KILNS processed quicklime to support the brick-building industry. And fossilized oyster shell was part of the prehistoric materials that formed rock.

OYSTER ROAST – The outdoor oyster roast has been a traditional lowcountry feast since before the arrival of the white man. In 1657, Spanish explorer Pedro Mendendez de Aviles wrote of the Edisto Indians preparing such a feast: "They lighted great fires [and] brought many shellfish . . . A great multitude of Indians came that night, and three chiefs . . . Many Indians came laden with corn, cooked and roasted fish, oysters and many acorns." The traditional way to steam oysters outside is to place them on a large piece of metal over a hot fire, placing a wet CROAKER SACK over them. This creates steam and allows the oysters to cook but also stay moist. (see CROAKER SACK)

PALMETTO – Three different palmettos are indigenous to coastal South Carolina, all distant relatives of the palm family. The dwarf palmetto (*Sabal minor*) is sometimes called the scrub palmetto and has short, fan-shaped leaves. Similar is the saw palmetto (*Serenoa repens*). The tall, palmetto tree (*Sabal palmetto*) is the South Carolina state tree, so designated for its role during the Battle of Fort Sullivan in 1776. (see FORT MOULTRIE)

PALMETTO GROVE – This LONG POINT plantation in CHRIST CHURCH PARISH was located on the WANDO RIVER between EGYPT PLANTATION and PARKER ISLAND. In the mid-1800s, it was owned by Dr. Edward Manly Royall (b. 1828). Palmetto Grove grew COTTON and provided beef, corn, and other subsistence crops for the Charleston market. There was also a substantial BRICKYARD here during the 18th and 19th centuries. Dr. Royall served in the CIVIL WAR as an assistant surgeon with the King's Battalion, Artillery, Longstreet's Corps. He was married to Ann Bailey VENNING and their son, Robert Venning Royall, was an intendant of MOUNT PLEASANT from 1898 to 1914. (see BRICKMAKING, LONG POINT, ROYALL AVENUE)

PALMETTO POINT – Point of land on the west side of Horlbeck Creek, location of Palmetto Islands County Park. An early map of the area marks this as the location of a Sewee Indian fort.

PARKER, ADMIRAL PETER (1721–1811) – Commander of the British naval forces at the Battle of Fort Sullivan, June 28, 1776. Parker's fleet included at least 50 ships, including transports, service vessels, and 9 men-of-war with a firepower that far exceeded WILLIAM MOULTRIE's meager armament at Fort Sullivan. During the battle, Admiral Parker (aboard the *Bristol*) was hit. His britches were "quite torn off, his backside laid bare, his thigh and knee wounded." Despite the British defeat in this action, Parker was later knighted for his bravery and eventually became admiral of the British fleet. (see HENRY CLINTON, WILLIAM MOULTRIE, REVOLUTIONARY WAR)

PARKER ISLAND – This island plantation in CHRIST CHURCH PARISH (on the WANDO RIVER where it meets Horlbeck Creek) was once the substantial BRICKYARD of Robert and Thomas Parker, *c.* 1850-60. It was later purchased by the Horlbeck family of BOONE HALL. (see BRICKMAKING)

PARRIS CREEK – A name given to SHEM CREEK, *c.* 1715, for Colonel Alexander Parris, who owned the adjacent lands. (see HOG ISLAND)

PATAPSCO, U.S.S. – On January 15, 1865, this Union monitor struck a Confederate torpedo and sank in the harbor in front of FORT MOULTRIE. Sixty-four officers and men aboard perished. A monument to this ship and these men is at the entrance to Fort Moultrie, adjacent to OSCEOLA's grave. (see CIVIL WAR)

PATJEN'S POST OFFICE – This quaint one-room clapboard building, now located off PITT STREET at Edwards Park in the OLD VILLAGE area of MOUNT PLEASANT, was originally erected *c.* 1899 on Church Street to serve as the Mount Pleasant post office. It was named for the Patjens family, postmasters during the early part of the 20th century. It was moved in 1971.

PATRIOT'S POINT – Located on HOG ISLAND, the major feature of this maritime museum is the aircraft carrier U.S.S. *Yorktown* and other military and civilian vessels. (see HOG ISLAND, MOUNT EDGECOMBE)

PELICAN – The South Carolina lowcountry is the largest nesting place for the brown pelican (*Pelecanus occidentalis*) in North America. These extremely large, prehistoric-looking birds have a wingspan of up to 7 feet and are distinctive for the throat pouch located under the bill. This pouch is not used for storing fish but for straining the water the bird takes in after a dive. The coastal Indians made tobacco pouches out of the pelican's throat pouch.

PEST HOUSE – Also called the LAZARETTO, this quarantine site on SULLIVAN'S ISLAND was first established in 1707. Erected on the southernmost tip of the island at THE COVE, the first pest house was built to quarantine immigrants coming from places known to have suffered epidemics of yellow fever. By 1744, a law was passed which required all slaves brought from Africa to be quarantined at the pest house for a period of ten days. Frequent hurricanes and storms damaged or destroyed the facility and, during the hurricane of 1752, the pest house was completely washed away, eventually making landfall at HOBCAW POINT. Miraculously, 9 of the 14 people inside the building survived. By 1770, a formal grievance was made against the poor conditions there and the *Gazette* wrote, "if the Pest House . . . was made tight, warm, comfortable . . . who would say, we wanted common Humanity?" By the early 1800s, the pest house was moved to Morris Island. Because it is thought that 40 percent of all the slaves brought to the United States performed quarantine at the pest house, Sullivan's Island has been dubbed the "Ellis Island of slavery." (see COUNTRY FEVER, DISEASE, GRACE-CHURCH, LAZARETTO, MOULTRIEVILLE, RESORT, SLAVERY, STRANGER'S FEVER)

PHOSPHATE MINING – In the late 1800s, phosphate mining and preparation became a major lowcountry industry and there were 15 phosphate works in Charleston. A remainder of prehistoric times, phosphate beds are ore rich in calcium and other minerals and were found throughout the lowcountry's tidal basins. Formed from the fossilized remains of mastodon and other prehistoric creatures, phosphate rock was described by a writer in 1877 as being, "hard like any other rock, overlying the river beds to an average thickness of eight inches to a foot . . . It is of a dark greenish-brown, and is full of fossil bones of mammoths, 'monsters of the slime' of other ages, and oyster shells of enormous size." High in lime content, phosphate was a natural and a potent fertilizer. It was processed and shipped out to points across the globe. The phosphate industry almost single-handedly brought Charleston out of the severe economic depression that followed the CIVIL WAR.

PIERATES CRUZ – Once a private home in MOUNT PLEASANT overlooking the harbor just south of ALHAMBRA HALL, Pierates Cruz was known for its lush gardens of azaleas and camellias. The name was a fanciful creation invented by the owners, Mr. and Mrs. Dana Osgood, who built Pierates Cruz in the 1920s. It is now a small residential development. (see OLD VILLAGE)

PILOTS – Harbor pilots were vital to shipping from the very beginning of the colony. They knew the intricacies of the harbor entrance and the ever-shifting sand shoals that could make entrance difficult prior to the building of the JETTIES and in the days of sail. Pilots were first organized at the lookout on SULLIVAN'S ISLAND in the 1680s. In 1723, John Hogg, Jonathan Collins, John Smith, and John Watson were ordered "to keep a sufficient number of good decked boats, well fitted with substantial tackle, rigging and apparel for the sea, and also necessary and proper canoes or boats . . . able and fitting to row out to sea . . . manned with one good and able person, besides the pilot and his apprentice or servant; and . . . shall (with a pilot on board) every day go over the Bar . . . to discover and go on board any ship or vessel intending for this port." Pilots are still required to board each vessel entering in or going out of the harbor. (see COASTAL WATCH, COPPER BUOYS, CROSSING THE BAR)

PINCKNEY FAMILY – Owners of SNEE FARM Plantation and SHELL HALL (located near present-day ALHAMBRA HALL). Historian Anne King GREGORIE wrote, "William Pinckney (b. 1704) married Robert Brewton's daughter, Ruth, and resided in the Parish." His son was Colonel Charles Pinckney (1732–1782), who purchased SNEE FARM in 1754. His son was "Constitution" Charles Pinckney (1758–1824). Cousins Thomas Pinckney (1750–1828) and Charles Cotesworth Pinckney (1746–1825) were the sons of Governor Charles Pinckney (1699–1758) and ELIZA LUCAS. Charles Cotesworth Pinckney served as an aide-de-camp to General Washington at Brandywine. In 1783, he was promoted to brigadier general; he was a delegate to the Constitutional Convention and later became minister to France in 1796. CASTLE PINCKNEY was named in his honor. (see SNEE FARM; also ALHAMBRA HALL, CASTLE PINCKNEY, HAMPTON, REVOLUTIONARY WAR, SHELL HALL, SHUTE'S FOLLY, WASHO)

PIRATES – The many inlets and bays of the BARRIER ISLANDS from CAPE ROMAIN to Charleston harbor were excellent hideaways for pirates to go ashore for fresh water or find a sandbar at low tide to careen their vessels and clean the hulls. In the late 1600s and early 1700s, pirates enjoyed a rather easy coexistence with the colony at CHARLES TOWN since they brought in badly needed hard currency and items for trade. This stopped, however, when the pirates began attacking vessels bound for or leaving the city. BLACKBEARD, STEDE BONNET, ANNE BONNEY, Calico Jack Rackam, Christopher Moody, and others were among the pirates who plundered Carolina waters. (see BLACKBEARD, STEDE BONNET, ANNE BONNEY, BULL'S ISLAND, *THE GOLD BUG*, EDGAR ALLAN POE, WILLIAM RHETT)

PITT STREET – This MOUNT PLEASANT street runs through the main "business" district of the OLD VILLAGE. When GREENWICH VILLAGE was established in the 1760s, the street was named to honor British Prime Minister William Pitt, who had openly argued in Parliament against the unfair taxes levied on the Americans. With over 50 years of service, the Pitt Street Pharmacy continues in operation, one of the few pharmacies remaining with an active soda fountain. (see BERKELEY COUNTY, DARBY BUILDING, OLD VILLAGE, PATJEN'S POST OFFICE, REVOLUTIONARY WAR, ST. PAUL'S LUTHERAN CHURCH)

PLANTATION – The word given in the 18th century for both new colonies and the farms established therein. The typical EAST COOPER plantation was not an elaborate "Tara" but a working farm of usually between 100 and 300 acres. Almost entirely self-sufficient and much like a small town, plantations grew their own food and produced as many of the necessary subsistence items as possible. Life centered around a main house, with a "street" leading up to it. The street was fronted by the slave cabins, and surrounded by outbuildings that housed the cooper, blacksmith, tanner, commissary, smokehouse, and kitchen. BOONE HALL is a prime example of this arrangement. In 1821, Samuel Sitgreaves visited the lowcountry and described the plantations as "islands in a sea of forest," since woods, rivers, creeks, marshes, and swamps placed very real geographic barriers between even neighboring plantations. (see CONCISE HISTORY; also GULLAH, SLAVERY)

PLANTER – Built at JONES SHIPYARD on SHEM CREEK for the plantation trade, this shallow-draft steamer became a BLOCKADE RUNNER for the Confederacy during the CIVIL WAR. The *Planter* became part of the Federal blockading fleet when, on the evening of May 13, 1862, the ship's officers went ashore, leaving Robert Smalls and the all-black crew aboard. Smalls seized the opportunity and made a run for the Union ships just outside the harbor entrance. Smalls and his crew were eventually awarded with prize money for their actions. (see BLOCKADE RUNNING, CIVIL WAR, JONES SHIPYARD)

PLANTER'S HOTEL – On SULLIVAN'S ISLAND in MOULTRIEVILLE in the early 1800s. An advertisement in the September 7, 1818 *Southern Patriot* announced, "PLANTER'S HOTEL, SULLIVAN'S ISLAND. The subscriber will open his HOUSE, on the first of June, for Visitors and constant Boarders. He pledges himself that the best Charleston and the Island Markets afford, shall always be provided. His Wines and Liquors shall be of the best quality. For the amusement of Visitors, two very elegant Billiard Tables are provided in a large, spacious and cool room. Chairs and Carriages will be provided for those who may wish to ride on the Island. ORRAN BYRD." (see CHENEY'S BOARDING HOUSE)

PLOUGH MUD – Also spelled *pluff* and pronounced like the word "enough," the name for the marsh mud which lines lowcountry salt marshes and creeks. In the late 18th and early 19th century, this nutrient-rich marsh mud was used as fertilizer. The mud was plowed into the soil, hence the word *plough*, an archaic spelling of *plow*. (see OYSTERS, SPARTINA)

POCOSIN – Along with the *SAPPHO*, this steam ferry was operated by the MOUNT PLEASANT FERRY COMPANY in the late 1800s. The *Pocosin*'s long career ended in 1893, when she grounded on the rocks of the GRILLAGE near SULLIVAN'S ISLAND.

POE, EDGAR ALLAN (1809–1849) – This famous American writer served at FORT MOULTRIE from 1827 to 1829 under the alias "Edgar A. Perry." Although his story *THE GOLD BUG* was written much later, he set the locale on SULLIVAN'S ISLAND. He also used the Charleston area as backdrop for two other works, "The Balloon Hoax" and "The Oblong Box." There is speculation that his poem "Annabelle Lee" might have been about a girl he met while stationed at Fort Moultrie and that the "kingdom by the sea" was Sullivan's Island or Charleston. The wind that "came out of a cloud by night/Chilling and killing my Annabel Lee" could refer to the many DISEASES that plagued Charleston during

that time. Some believe Annabelle Lee was a kinswoman of DR. EDMUND
RAVENEL. Some also believe that Dr. Ravenel was the model for the protagonist,
Legrand, in *THE GOLD BUG*. (see MYRTLES)

POINT HOUSE – This hotel was located at MOULTRIEVILLE on the
southernmost point of SULLIVAN'S ISLAND in the 1800s. The Point House
was lost in the hurricane of 1854. (see HURRICANE ALLEY)

POMPION HILL – This small Episcopal CHAPEL OF EASE serving ST.
THOMAS PARISH was originally built of cypress in 1703. The present brick
chapel was built in 1761. The word *pompion* is an archaic English word for pumpkin,
and Pompion Hill is locally pronounced as "Punkin' Hill." Pompion Hill Plantation,
established by HUGUENOT émigré Pierre de St. Julien de Malacare (1669–1718)
in the 1680s, was the original name of the plantation adjacent to the chapel. The
plantation name was changed to LONGWOOD in 1823. Services are still held
at Pompion Hill chapel twice a year, in the spring and fall. (see EAST BRANCH,
CHAPEL OF EASE, FRENCH QUARTER, HUGUENOTS, LONGWOOD,
MIDDLEBURG, QUINBY BARONY, RAVENEL)

POOR JOE – From the African word *pojo*, which means "heron," it is the GULLAH
term for a heron or egret.

PORCHER – The patriarch of the Porcher family in South Carolina was
HUGUENOT émigré Dr. Isaac Porcher (pronounced *Po-shay*), who came to
Carolina *c.* 1699, "born in France, Province of Berry, town of Saints Seuerre." The
Porcher family established plantations along the mainland overlooking COPAHEE
SOUND, which became known as PORCHER's Bluff. These included the
plantations called YOUGHALL, LAUREL HILL, and OAKLAND. Subsequent
members of the Porcher family married with other CHRIST CHURCH
PARISH families, most notably the Bonneau, DuPré, Cordes, DuBose, Gaillard,
GREGORIE, and VENNING families. Philip Edward Porcher (1827–1917), the
son of Philip Porcher and Martha DuBose, was the engineer in charge of erecting
the CONFEDERATE LINES in CHRIST CHURCH PARISH. (see BONNEAU
BEACH, GENERAL JAMES CHAPLIN BEECHER, GREGORIE, OAKLAND,
POTTER'S RAIDERS, TIPPYCUTLAW, VENNING, YOUGHALL)

PORT ROYALL – One of the three original ships bound for CAROLINA in 1670, the
Port Royall (named for the original destination of the colonists) was wrecked during a
storm in the Bahamas and never made it to Carolina. Her passengers, however, were
saved. (see CONCISE HISTORY; also *CAROLINA*

POTTER'S RAIDERS – GENERAL SHERMAN's arm in lower South
Carolina, these Union troops served under the command of Brigadier General
Edward E. Potter after the Union occupation of Charleston. Potter's troops

earned the sobriquet "Potter's Raiders" for the sometimes wanton destruction of property and were, in large part, responsible for the widespread looting and burning of lowcountry plantations. (see ANDERSONVILLE CUT, CIVIL WAR, LIMERICK, OAKLAND PLANTATION, PORCHER)

POYAS, MRS. (ANCIENT LADY) – Under the pseudonym "Ancient Lady," Elizabeth Ann Scott, the daughter of William Scott of SCOTT'S FERRY and the wife of RICE planter Henry Poyas, published several gossipy historical pamphlets on the people and history of the Cooper River plantations. Her most notable work was entitled "The Olden Times in Carolina." (see THE BLESSING, GENERAL SHERMAN; also BIBLIOGRAPHY)

PRESTO – This Confederate BLOCKADE RUNNER was a sidewheel steamer that ran aground on the GRILLAGE at SULLIVAN'S ISLAND on the night of February 2, 1864. (see BLOCKADE RUNNING, GRILLAGE)

PRIOLI – Name given to BONNEAU FERRY Plantation during its ownership by the Prioleau family. (see EAST BRANCH)

PRIVATEER – The name generally given to an armed vessel, owned privately, which sailed under a letter of marque in the service of one country to cruise against war vessels of an enemy country. Several famous privateers were built at HOBCAW for the War of 1812, most notably the 240-ton schooner, *Stephen Decatur*, the 170-ton *Saucy Jack*, and the corvette, *John Adams*. Privateering was abolished in the United States in 1856. (see SHIPYARD PLANTATION)

QUELCH, BENJAMIN – From BARBADOS, on February 23, 1681, Quelch purchased a plantation of 330 acres of land "on E side Wando River," becoming one of the earliest owners of HOBCAW Plantation and the shipyard there. He was married to Richard Dearsley's sister, Elizabeth. (see DEARSLEY'S CREEK, HOBCAW POINT, MOLASSES CREEK, SHIPYARD PLANTATION, WAKENDAW, WAPPETAW)

QUELCH'S CREEK – An early name given to WAKENDAW Creek during the ownership of BENJAMIN QUELCH in the late 1600s. (see COINBOW CREEK)

QUINBY (QUENBY) BARONY, CREEK, PLANTATION – In 1681, John Ashby was granted 2,000 acres on the eastern shore of the headwaters of the Cooper River's EAST BRANCH, "at a place called by the Indians Yadhaw." Ashby, a merchant from London, was the younger son of Sir George Ashby of Quenby, Leicestershire, hence the name for his CAROLINA plantation. The area and creek are variously spelled as *Quinby*, *Quimby*, *Quenby*, and *Queen Bee*. Landholders of this RICE plantation included Thomas Shubrick, Thomas PINCKNEY, and members of the Ball family. The original plantation house, erected *c.* 1792, was moved to

HALIDON HILL in 1954. (see BARONY, EAST BRANCH, HALIDON HILL, HUGER, PINCKNEY, YADHAW)

QUINBY BRIDGE, BATTLE OF – The bridge spanning Quinby Creek, a tributary of the Cooper River's EAST BRANCH, located just to the west of the crossroads community of HUGER. Here, on July 17, 1781, General Thomas Sumter, commanding 700 men, fought a British force of 600 men. Sixty Americans were killed or wounded; British casualties numbered 145. In the annals of ST. THOMAS PARISH, it was written that "those who fell were buried by the roadside." This common grave mound is still seen lining the hill between the avenue of oaks at QUINBY PLANTATION and the bridge. (see REVOLUTIONARY WAR)

RACCOON – This nocturnal mammal (*Procyon lotor*) is known for its habit of washing its food before eating and *lotor*, loosely translated, means "washer." Approximately 3 feet long, with a long snout and a bushy, ringed tail, the raccoon dines on oysters, clams, mussels, frogs, small reptiles, fish, and, in residential areas, dinner taken from a raided garbage can. Raccoons generally sleep in the day and forage at night in familial groups. The word comes from the Algonkian Indian word, *arahkun*.

RACCOON KEY – Island at the north end of BULL'S BAY at CAPE ROMAIN, also known as LIGHTHOUSE ISLAND. (see CAPE ROMAIN)

RAVENEL – The patriarch of this prominent lowcountry family was HUGUENOT émigré, René Ravenel (b. 1656). In 1689, he married Charlotte de St. Julien at POMPION HILL. Ravenel descendants had landholdings in ST. JAMES SANTEE, CHRIST CHURCH, ST. THOMAS, and ST. JOHN'S Parishes. In 1719, his son Daniel Ravenel (1692–1736) built the first house at 68 Broad Street, and the later house erected on the site *c.* 1796 is the oldest residential property in Charleston to remain continuously in the same family. Ravenel descendants include Dr. EDMUND RAVENEL and DR. HENRY WILLIAM RAVENEL. Senator Arthur P. Ravenel, for whom the new COOPER RIVER BRIDGE is named, is also a descendant. (see FRENCH SANTEE, HUGUENOTS, LONGWOOD, POMPION HILL.)

RAVENEL, DR. EDMUND (1797–1871) – Esteemed both for his medical abilities as well as for his discoveries as a naturalist, Dr. Ravenel began summering on SULLIVAN'S ISLAND in 1823, where he began one of the most complete collection of marine shells ever compiled. He eventually catalogued (and in some instances, named) over 3,500 specimens. His scientific studies brought him into contact with DR. LOUIS AGASSIZ, JOHN JAMES AUDUBON, DR. JOHN BACHMAN, and other naturalists of the period. On several occasions he was in charge of the hospital at FORT MOULTRIE and, in 1858, when yellow fever caused a general migration to Sullivan's Island, he was Intendant of MOULTRIEVILLE. A firm believer in the healing powers of the seaside, he penned *The Advantages of a Sea-Shore Residence in the Treatment of Certain Diseases, and the Therapeutic Employment of Sea-Water*, published in 1850. Some literary historians believe EDGAR ALLAN POE used Dr. Ravenel as the model for Legrand in *THE GOLD BUG*. Along with his summer residence on the island, Ravenel had a town house in Charleston and plantation lands, including THE GROVE on the COOPER RIVER. (see DR. LOUIS AGASSIZ, JOHN JAMES AUDUBON, FRENCH SANTEE, THE GROVE, FRENCH SANTEE, HUGUENOTS, SULLIVAN'S ISLAND)

RAVENEL, DR. HENRY WILLIAM (1790–1867) – Dr. Ravenel's home was Pooshee Plantation in upper ST. JOHN'S PARISH. Although he studied medicine in Charleston and Philadelphia, he gave up his medical practice in 1824 to devote full time to the management of RICE, becoming widely published for the innovations he developed regarding rice farming. His accomplishments as a botanist earned him national and international recognition. Like other planters, Ravenel summered on SULLIVAN'S ISLAND, and JOHN JAMES AUDUBON visited him there in the summer of 1831. He was also a colleague of DR. JOHN BACHMAN and his kinsman, DR. EDMUND RAVENEL.

READ, DR. BENJAMIN (1753–1845) – This REVOLUTIONARY WAR hero and physician was once an owner of RICE HOPE plantation on the upper COOPER RIVER. He served as deputy surgeon general under General George Washington and, under orders from Washington, is purported to have ridden from New Jersey to South Carolina in a record 18 days "on his own horse and entirely at his own expense." (see HUGER, WEST BRANCH)

REBELLION ROAD – In marine terms, a "road" is a safe anchorage. Rebellion Road, in the harbor just off the NORTH POINT of MOUNT PLEASANT, has been a safe anchorage for ships since the settlement of the colony. In the late 1600s, all vessels entering the harbor were required to anchor here and make their business known to the colonial governor. Not to do so meant the ship was in "rebellion," hence the name. (see CROSSING THE BAR, PILOTS)

REMLEY'S POINT – In MOUNT PLEASANT, the point of land between HOBCAW and HOG ISLAND (PATRIOT'S POINT). Paul D. Remley (d. 1863) left a will that, despite the difficult political environment, ensured that his black slaves not only gained freedom, but also inherited his land. The present boat landing was once a park and beach known as Mosquito Beach.

RESORTS – "The inhabitants, compelled to leave their estates in May . . . are forced to lead a wretched wandering life," wrote Reverend Samuel Sitgreaves in 1821, barely overstating the effect disease had on the social order of the Carolina lowcountry. Englishman Francis Hall wrote in 1816, "all the inhabitants who can afford it, then fly to a barren sand-bank in the harbour, called Sullivan's Island." Each May, in order to escape the "bad air" of the inland swamps, plantation

families "resorted" to areas they considered more healthful. Areas along the
seashore were favored and, by the early 1800s, the summering communities of
SULLIVAN'S ISLAND, MOUNT PLEASANT, and McCLELLANVILLE
had been established. Here, they stayed until September or October, generally
until the mosquito season had ended. (see DISEASE, COUNTRY FEVER,
STRANGER'S FEVER)

REVOLUTIONARY WAR – The era of the American Revolution (1764–
1792) was one that pitted brother against brother in the CHARLES TOWN
area. The wealthy plantation society had strong family ties with Great Britain;
many of the same men who would become staunch Patriots had been educated
there. Yet after the passage of the unfair Sugar Act in 1764, followed by the
Stamp Act in 1765, open dissension soon replaced even familial loyalty. William
Pitt, who made an open plea before Parliament against the Stamp Act and in
behalf of the colonies, became a hero. A statue was erected in his honor and
streets were named for him, such as PITT STREET in MOUNT PLEASANT.
After the passage of the Tea Act, Charlestonians staged the first "tea party" on
November 3, 1773, throwing seven chests of tea into the harbor with Boston
following suit a month later. In January 1774, a Council of Safety was formed,
followed by the First Provincial Congress. On November 11–12, 1775, during
what became known as the BATTLE OF HOG ISLAND CHANNEL, the
South Carolina schooner *Defense* successfully engaged the H.M.S. *Tamar* and
H.M.S. *Cherokee*. On June 28, 1776, the Battle of Fort Sullivan occurred on
SULLIVAN'S ISLAND, with Americans under WILLIAM MOULTRIE
routing a powerful fleet of warships under General SIR HENRY CLINTON.
A week later, the Declaration of Independence was signed, with Thomas
Lynch jr. of HOPSEWEE and LYNCH'S GROVE being one of the signers.
HENRY LAURENS of MEPKIN served as a president of the Continental
Congress. After the fall of Charles Town in 1780, HADDRELL'S POINT
(now the OLD VILLAGE area) was made a prisoner-of-war camp; WILLIAM
MOULTRIE and Charles PINCKNEY of SNEE FARM were among those
held here. Others were held in the prison ships *CONCORD*, *PACKHORSE*, and
TABAR anchored in the harbor. Despite British control of Charles Town, the
outlying areas were still open, and numerous skirmishes took place throughout
1781–82. British troops under Colonel Banestre Tarleton, called "Bloody
Tarleton" for his barbarities, began terrorizing inland farms and plantations.
Their looting, burning of homes, and indiscriminate killing brought many
previously uninvolved citizens to take up arms. FRANCIS MARION formed
his partisan rangers and harassed the British with guerilla tactics, escaping into
the wilds of places like HELL HOLE SWAMP. Even after LORD CHARLES
CORNWALLIS surrendered at Yorktown, skirmishes continued, including
BIGGIN'S BRIDGE, VIDEAU BRIDGE, and, on August 29, 1782, at
WADBOO PLANTATION. Finally, in December 1782, the British capitulated
and evacuated Charles Town.

RHETT, COLONEL WILLIAM (1666–1723) – One of the wealthiest and, except for his father-in-law, Judge Nicholas Trott, perhaps the most important man in CHARLES TOWN during the proprietary period. Rhett was also the colony's principal military man, successfully leading the colonial militia against warring Indians, the FRENCH-SPANISH INVASION, and pirates like STEDE BONNET, whom he apprehended in 1719. In 1713, after a hurricane destroyed the tower on SULLIVAN'S ISLAND and no public monies were available to rebuild it, Rhett used his own money to erect a new brick tower on the island. He was married to Mary Trott. (see AHAGAN, COASTAL WATCH, CROSSING THE BAR, LOOKOUTS, THE HAGAN, FRENCH-SPANISH INVASION, PIRATES)

RICE – Possibly no other crop was as important to the culturally diverse history of CAROLINA than rice. Called Carolina Golden Rice and esteemed for its taste and smooth texture, rice was being exported from the colony prior to 1700. Thousands of tons of rice were shipped yearly from lowcountry plantations, ultimately creating one of the wealthiest societies in America. The French HUGUENOT planters devised an ingenious diking system that allowed them to harness the tidally influenced rivers to drain and flood the fields as needed. But rice was a labor-intensive crop, so slaves were brought specifically from the regions along the West African Grain Coast where rice had been grown for centuries. Their cultural influence remains an integral part of lowcountry society and is reflected in language, cuisine, and music. The unique SWEETGRASS BASKETS now sold as "show" baskets were originally created as work baskets for the rice plantations and are still used in Sierra Leone today. In the late 1700s, millwright JONATHAN LUCAS revolutionized the milling process with the invention of a steam-driven rice mill. Rice remained the primary crop until the CIVIL WAR. While the war changed dramatically the labor standard, planting was continued by a few planters afterwards with a modicum of success. These remaining fields were destroyed by a series of hurricanes in the late 1800s and early 1900s, marking the final demise of this once-great lowcountry crop. (see CONCISE HISTORY; also ABOVE THE SALTS, ASHLEY RIVER, EAST BRANCH, ECHAW, GEORGETOWN, GULLAH, HUGUENOTS, HENRY WILLIAM RAVENEL, SHEM CREEK, SLAVERY, WACAMAW, WASHO, WEST BRANCH)

RICE HOPE – This RICE plantation on the eastern shore of the COOPER RIVER is just above the TEE and adjacent to Strawberry. Granted to HUGUENOT émigré Daniel HUGER in 1696, it was originally known as Luckins. During its ownership by DR. BENJAMIN READ in the late 1700s and early 1800s, the land was cleared for extensive rice fields, and the plantation house, *c.* 1790, was built. The house was rebuilt in the 1840s and additions added in the 1920s. Rice Hope is now a 40-room inn and is open to the public. (see CHILDSBURY, WEST BRANCH)

RICHMOND PLANTATION – This former RICE plantation is on the western shore of the Cooper River's EAST BRANCH, between BOSSIS and BONNEAU FERRY. Originally established in the early 1700s by John Harleston, it was later owned by Edward Rutledge, the son of Governor John Rutledge. In the mid-1800s, it was the home of Dr. William Harleston Hugen(1826–1906), one of Charleston's most beloved physicians and sportsmen. The original plantation house burned in 1900. Now owned by the Girl Scouts, it is listed on the National Historic Register.

RIFLE RANGE ROAD – During World War I, the U.S. Navy leased 100 acres of land from George Goblet to build a rifle range for training northeast of MOUNT PLEASANT. Today, Rifle Range Road runs from Ben Sawyer Boulevard to PORCHER's Bluff.

RONKIN'S LONG ROOM – This tavern was in the OLD VILLAGE of MOUNT PLEASANT (1850s and 1860s) on the south side of FERRY STREET near the ferry house wharf. It was here, in 1860, that a public meeting was held to discuss the matter of secession. Eleven resolutions were drawn up, and it was agreed that if Abraham Lincoln were elected president, Mount Pleasant would support South Carolina's decision to secede from the Union.

ROSE'S SHIPYARD – John Rose's shipyard was one of the many located at HOBCAW POINT. In 1763, the 180-ton vessel *Heart of Oak*, launched from Rose's Shipyard, was the largest vessel ever built on the COOPER RIVER. (see SHIPYARD PLANTATION)

ROYALL AVENUE – This street, originally named COMMON STREET, runs parallel to PITT STREET and SIMMONS STREET in the OLD VILLAGE area of MOUNT PLEASANT. It was named for Robert VENNING Royall (1854–1935), mayor of Mount Pleasant from 1898 to 1914. (see PALMETTO GROVE)

RUTLEDGE, ARCHIBALD (1883–1973) – South Carolina's first poet laureate. Archibald Hamilton Rutledge's home was HAMPTON PLANTATION on the south SANTEE RIVER. Born in McCLELLANVILLE in 1883, Rutledge was the grandson of Frederick Rutledge and Harriott Pinckney Horry. Hampton was the ancestral home of the Horry family. Rutledge wrote both prose and poetry with an emphasis on nature and the South Carolina lowcountry, including the celebrated work, *Home by the River*, a collection of poetry on the beauty of the Santee River and its environs. At his death, he bequeathed Hampton to the state of South Carolina, and it is now a state park. (see ECHAW, ELIZA LUCAS, ST. JAMES SANTEE, WADMACON, WAMBAW)

ST. ANDREW'S EPISCOPAL CHURCH – In Mount Pleasant's OLD VILLAGE on ROYALL STREET, this congregation was originally organized in 1835 as a CHAPEL OF EASE for CHRIST CHURCH PARISH. The present neo-Gothic structure was erected in 1857. It continues to serve Mount Pleasant as an active Episcopal congregation.

ST. DENIS – Church near FRENCH QUARTER CREEK, erected prior to 1700, serving the French HUGUENOT settlers along the Cooper River's EAST BRANCH. It is likely that the name was chosen for the patron saint of France, St. Denis. The first minister was the Reverend Mr. John LePierre. After the passage of the CHURCH ACT of 1706, St. Denis was included in the parish of ST. THOMAS, and the church made a parish CHAPEL OF EASE. This act also stipulated that the congregation of St. Denis could worship in French. By 1755, most of the original French refugees in the parish were dead, and their descendants had united themselves with the Church of England. In 1768, an act was passed dissolving the French congregation and the church records, lands, buildings, and effects were given to the vestry of ST. THOMAS. Nothing remains of this early church, and its exact location is unknown. (see ORANGE QUARTER)

ST. JAMES MOUNTED RIFLEMEN – This Confederate unit from ST. JAMES SANTEE and CHRIST CHURCH PARISH was part of the Fifth South Carolina Cavalry, Company E, under Captain Louis Augustus WHILDEN and Captain William Capers VENNING. Their roster included Lieutenant Elias Venning, Second Lieutenant James Anderson, J.I. Inglesby, Nelson Byam, and R.K. Axson. (see ANDERSONVILLE, CIVIL WAR, VENNING, WHILDEN)

ST. JAMES SANTEE – Created by the CHURCH ACT of 1706, this parish generally covered the area from the South SANTEE RIVER to AWENDAW. The first parish church was a wooden structure in ECHAW; the present edifice, the fourth to be built, is known familiarly as the "Brick Church" and was constructed in 1768. Located on the old GEORGETOWN ROAD between McCLELLANVILLE and HAMPTON PLANTATION, it is on the National Historic Register. The cypress shingled church of St. James Santee-McClellanville was built in 1890 as a CHAPEL OF EASE for village inhabitants to use during the summer months.

ST. JOHN'S PARISH, BERKELEY – Created by the CHURCH ACT OF 1706, this parish was divided into upper and lower sections. The lower parish served the plantations on the Cooper River's WEST BRANCH; the parish church was at BIGGIN. At CHILDSBURY, the STRAWBERRY CHAPEL served as a parish CHAPEL OF EASE. (see BIGGIN, STRAWBERRY CHAPEL)

ST. PAUL'S LUTHERAN CHURCH – On PITT STREET in the OLD VILLAGE area of MOUNT PLEASANT, this church was erected in the 1890s to serve the growing German population of that time. A simple white clapboard with central steeple and red door, it was designed to resemble a typical German village church. The original church sat 125; a new church was erected in 1972 and the chapel now serves as the parish hall. (see OCEAN GROVE CEMETERY)

ST. THOMAS CHURCH – The first St. Thomas Church was finished in 1708, "built of brick . . . on a neck of land, on the N.W. side of Wando River," and adjoined by 200 acres of glebe lands. In 1709, the Reverend Thomas Hasell was sent as a missionary to the parish. The original church was destroyed by fire in 1815. The present church dates to 1819. (see BERESFORD BOUNTY, CAINHOY, CHAPEL OF EASE, POMPION HILL)

ST. THOMAS PARISH – Created by the CHURCH ACT of 1706, this parish generally covered the area from DANIEL ISLAND to the headwaters of the Cooper River's EAST BRANCH. With the addition of the French HUGUENOT church of ST. DENIS in the FRENCH QUARTER, it became known as the parish of ST. THOMAS & ST DENIS. The parish church was ST. THOMAS CHURCH. POMPION HILL was the parish's CHAPEL OF EASE.

SALT HOPE/SALT PONDS – These contiguous plantations near AWENDAW were originally part of the 12,000-acre SEWEE BARONY, granted to Governor Nathaniel Johnson in the 1696. The lands were located on the south of Awendaw Creek and fronted Sewee Bay. Salt Hope comprised 1,040 acres; Salt Ponds, 1,100 acres. The *Journals of the Grand Council* of August 20, 1716, refers to a letter sent to Captain Thomas Lynch "to be left at Mr. Benjamin Webb's at the Salt Ponds near Seawee." It was later owned by Gabriel MANIGAULT and his descendants. During his Southern Tour in 1791, President George Washington lodged at the main plantation house, then under the ownership of Joseph Manigault. (see LYNCH'S GROVE, SILK HOPE)

SAN MIGUEL DE GUALDAPE – Name of the unsuccessful settlement attempted near present-day Georgetown by the Spanish in 1526. (see ALLYON)

SANTEE/SANTEE RIVER– The Siouan tribe who lived along the Santee River from the coast to the present town of Santee. The name possibly comes from the word *iswan'ti*, meaning "river" or "the river is here."

SAPPHO – This harbor steam ferry made her inaugural run on June 28, 1876, as part of the centennial celebration of the Battle of Fort Sullivan. Touted as "the swift and elegant sidewheel steamer *Sappho*," she was a steam-driven one-ender with huge paddle wheels. She was well loved and appreciated for her idiosyncratic creaks, groans, and shudders, which delighted locals but could initially alarm first-time passengers. During the summer months, the *Sappho* made six trips daily between SULLIVAN'S ISLAND and town, except on Sundays, when the number was reduced to five. The *Sappho* was retired in 1926 after 50 years of operation. (see *CYPRESS*, MOUNT PLEASANT FERRY COMPANY, *POCOSIN*)

SCOTT, JONATHAN – Developer of GREENWICH VILLAGE in the 1760s, Scott also owned a mill on the upper reaches of SHEM CREEK as well as a tavern at Scott's Corner. Like many Englishmen living in Charleston at the time, Scott remained loyal to the Crown during the Revolutionary War and returned to England in 1782.

SCOTT'S FERRY – Later known as CLEMENT'S FERRY, this ferry joining DANIEL ISLAND to the Charleston Neck was invested to Joseph Scott in 1765. (see CALAIS AND DOVER FERRY, POYAS)

SCOTT'S TAVERN – Owned by JONATHAN SCOTT, the developer of GREENWICH VILLAGE in the 1760s, this tavern was located at Scott's Corner, the junction of the GEORGETOWN ROAD and the road that led from MOUNT PLEASANT to HOBCAW. (see INNS & TAVERNS)

SEA OATS – The tall oat-like grass (*Uniola paniculata*) seen on beach sand dunes. Each sea oat plant has a complex root system that extends far beneath the sand and helps stabilize the ever-shifting sand of the dunes. So important are the sea oats to the dunes environment that it is against the law to pick them. (see BARRIER ISLAND)

SEASIDE LABORATORY – Established by DR. LOUIS AGASSIZ on SULLIVAN'S ISLAND in 1851 to study mollusks (shells) and other marine life. Agassiz had three full-time assistants working at this laboratory located in MOULTRIEVILLE. In a letter written to botanist James D. Dana, January 26, 1852, Agassiz described his work on the island: "Mr. Clark, one of my assistants, has made very good drawings of all stages of growth of hydroid medusae peculiar to this coast. Mr. Stimpson, another very promising young naturalist, who has been connected with me for some time in the same capacity, draws the crustacea and bryozoa, of which are also a good many new ones here. My son and my old friend Burkhardt are also with me upon Sullivan's Island, and they look after the larger species." William Smith Clark (1826–1886) went on to become president of the Massachusetts Agricultural College and was also instrumental in the establishment of the Imperial College of Agriculture in Sapporo, Japan. William Stimpson (1832–1872) was later curator of the Chicago Academy of Sciences. James Burkhardt was an artist who had accompanied Agassiz on his expeditions in South America. Alexander Agassiz, his son, continued his father's work and was a fellow at Harvard until 1885. Agassiz kept this laboratory until 1853. (see BACHMAN, RAVENEL)

SEASIDE PLANTATION – Also called Seaside Farms, this plantation overlooking HAMLIN SOUND off RIFLE RANGE ROAD was in the Whitesides family by 1755, when Thomas Whitesides was a vestryman at Christ Church. At his death, the property went to his five sons, Thomas, John, William, Edward, and Moses Whitesides. The plantation initially grew RICE and later provided meat, corn, potatoes, and other subsistence crops for the Charleston market. Part of the property was sold in 1859 to Peter Porcher Bonneau, and he established a salt works on the property. (see BONNEAU BEACH)

SEEWEE BARONY – Also known as AWENDAW Barony. Governor Sir Nathaniel Johnson was granted "12,000 acres on Auendaubooe Creek" as a barony in 1709. Included in this grant were adjoining tracts granted to Johnson in 1696, SALT PONDS, and SALT HOPE, which was 600 acres "to the Northeast side of Sewee Bay." In 1763, 5,145 acres were conveyed to his descendant Gabriel MANIGAULT and remained in the Manigault family until the late 1800s. President George Washington visited here during his Southern Tour in 1791 when the property was in the possession of Joseph Manigault. The lands are generally in the same location as the SEWEE village the original colonists visited after their arrival in 1670. (see CONCISE HISTORY; also AWENDAW, BARONY, MANIGAULT)

SEWEE (SEEWEE) INDIANS – A tribe of the Siouan linguistic group, the Sewees lived along the coast from Charleston harbor to the SANTEE RIVER with a main village near AWENDAW. The name probably means either "island" or "island people." These were the people who greeted the first English colonists landing at BULL'S ISLAND in 1670. The entire tribe was almost obliterated when they attempted to go to England in canoes to trade their deerskins directly with the English king, thus eliminating the colonial traders as middle men. They were barely out of sight of land when hit by a fierce hurricane. Most drowned, and the unfortunate survivors were picked up by a passing vessel and sold into slavery in the Caribbean. By 1715, according to one contemporary source, the Sewees had "but one village of 57 souls." (see CONCISE HISTORY; also BULL'S ISLAND, CAPER'S ISLAND, COASTAL WATCHES, CUSABO, DEWEES ISLAND, GEORGETOWN ROAD, HUNTING ISLANDS, SHELL MIDDENS)

SEEWEE RIVER – Name variously given to AWENDAW Creek in the 18th century.

SHARK HOLE – This remarkably deep (80 feet) hole is located where the INTRACOASTAL WATERWAY merges with Dewees Inlet and is noted for its excellent fishing, particularly shark fishing.

SHE-CRAB – The colloquial and GULLAH name for a female BLUE CRAB. Females are marked with distinct ridges on the V-shaped apron on their underbelly, and when they are carrying eggs, the apron is open and underneath is seen an orange mass called the "sponge." While it is illegal to harvest female blue crabs carrying sponges, often when they are cleaned there is roe inside, a bright orange gelatinous substance. The term "she-crab soup" comes from the addition of this roe to the soup.

SHELL HALL – The summer home of the PINCKNEY family of SNEE FARM, it was located on the MOUNT PLEASANT waterfront near present-day ALHAMBRA HALL. (see ALHAMBRA HALL, DISEASE, PINCKNEY, RESORT)

SHELL MIDDENS, SHELL RINGS or SHELL MOUNDS – These circular structures, composed entirely of shell refuse (oyster, clam, and conch), once dotted the entire coastline, a remnant of the former Indian inhabitants. Some ethnologists are of the opinion that these heaps were nothing more than refuse dumps, a result of the large number of shellfish in the diet of the coastal Indians. Others feel that their often-uniform proportions were purposely designed and they were likely erected for ceremonial purposes, either for religious ceremonies or as a place for astronomical observations. Few shell rings still exist, as most were plundered by the early colonists to pave roads or to make lime for use in the construction of buildings and fortifications. One of the largest still intact today is the Great Sewee Shell Ring, 300 feet in circumference, 40 feet wide, and 9 feet thick. Located just south of AWENDAW off Doar Road, it is open to the public, accessible by a nature trail. (see LIME KILN, ISLE OF PALMS, OLD FORT, SEWEE INDIANS)

SHEM CREEK – The name originates with the Indian word *Shemee* (meaning unknown, although ethnologists believe adding the "ee" to a word indicated a watercourse, such as Santee, Wampee, Wateree, etc.) It is first mentioned in the will of John GODFREY (d. 1689), when he refers to "my land near Shembee." As late as 1784, it was still referred to as Shemee when John Scott purchased 471 acres "northeast of Shamee Creek." Other names have been given to the creek depending upon ownership of adjoining lands, and it has been variously called SULLIVAN'S, Dearsley's, Rowser's, Parris, and Lemprier's Creek. Various businesses relating to ships and shipbuilding have been on the creek. A LIME KILN was located here in the 1760s. Also, JONATHAN LUCAS erected the first water-driven RICE mill here. Since the early 1900s, it has been the center of the commercial seafood industry for Charleston. (see CONCISE HISTORY; also ADDISON'S SHIPYARD, BUCKET FACTORY, COOTER, FACTORY STREET, FRENCH-SPANISH INVASION, HADDRELL'S POINT, HALL'S SHIPYARD, HIBBEN, HOG ISLAND, JONES SHIPYARD, JUGNOT & HILLIARD, LIME KILN, JONATHAN LUCAS, MAGWOOD, MASTODON BONES, MILL STREET, OLD VILLAGE, *PLANTER*, JONATHAN SCOTT, VILLEPONTOUX)

SHERMAN, GENERAL WILLIAM TECUMSEH (1820–1891) – Not the most popular person in lowcountry history for his scorched-earth policy, which destroyed so many Southern plantations during the CIVIL WAR, Sherman had previously established friendships here when he served at FORT MOULTRIE in 1842. He befriended Colonel Jacob Bond I'on while on the island. He also broke his arm during a hunting expedition on the Cooper River's EAST BRANCH with members of the POYAS family. Some feel that one reason many of the plantations east of the Cooper River were saved from the torch during the Federal occupation was because of Sherman's fondness for the area and the kindness people had shown him during his time at Fort Moultrie. (see CONCISE HISTORY; also ANDERSONVILLE, CIVIL WAR, POTTER'S RAIDERS, POYAS)

SHIPYARD PLANTATION – Plantation at HOBCAW, so named for the shipyards located here. Established in the late 1600s, it is considered to be the oldest shipyard in America. This point was heavily wooded with pine, oak, and ash and also had deepwater access. (see CONCISE HISTORY; also BLOCKADE RUNNING, *CAROLINA PACKET*, HOBCAW, PRIVATEER, BENJAMIN QUELCH, ROSE'S SHIPYARD)

SHUTE'S FOLLY – The island in the harbor on which the ruins of CASTLE PINCKNEY stand. The island, then much larger (224 acres), was originally granted to Alexander Parris in 1711. In 1746, it was deeded to Joseph Shute and became known as Shute's Folly for its lush vegetation. Shute also had a sizable ORANGE Grove on the island. In 1805, 50 acres on the island were purchased by JONATHAN LUCAS, and he may have erected a rice milling operation there. (see FOLLY, ORANGES.)

SILK HOPE – This former RICE plantation at the headwaters of the Cooper River's EAST BRANCH was originally granted to Governor Nathaniel Johnson, who experimented with silk production here, thus its name. In 1739, when the property was owned by Gabriel MANIGAULT, it comprised some 5,000 acres. It remained in that family until the late 1800s. (see CYPRESS BARONY, EAST BRANCH, FRENCH/SPANISH INVASION, SALT HOPE/SALT PONDS, SEEWEE BARONY)

SIMMONS STREET – Once known as BOUNDARY STREET, since it formed the northern boundary of the OLD VILLAGE of MOUNT PLEASANT, it was renamed to honor Yonge Simmons, who served as mayor of Mount Pleasant in 1916 and from 1921 to 1928.

SIXTEEN-MILE HOUSE – Located just beyond the WAPPETAW MEETING HOUSE, this commodious inn on the GEORGETOWN ROAD was frequented during the REVOLUTIONARY WAR by both British and American troops. (see INNS & TAVERNS, WAPPETAW)

SLAVERY – To support the labor-intensive RICE plantations, African slaves, brought primarily from the rice-growing region of Sierra Leone and Gambia, came into colonial CAROLINA by the thousands. As early as 1710, slaves comprised more than half of the colony's population; by the late 1730s, an estimated 2,400 African slaves were imported annually. This soon led to a solid black majority.

The ratio of blacks to whites could be has high as 19-to-1 in rice- and INDIGO-producing areas. The population of CHRIST CHURCH PARISH in 1800 was 432 whites compared to 3,585 African slaves; in ST. THOMAS PARISII, it was 207 whites to 2,328 African slaves. Not everyone owned slaves; not every slave owner was white. Free blacks also owned slaves in South Carolina. While the average number of slaves on an east of the Cooper PLANTATION was usually less than 20, a large rice plantation could need as many as 200 hands. Not all slaves were field hands. Artisans with special skills supported the building, BRICKMAKING, and shipbuilding trades. Because of the solid black majority and the relative isolation of the plantation, much of the original African culture and language survived, seen particularly in the language called GULLAH. Of the estimated 12–15 million Africans sold into slavery, an estimated 500,000 (approximately 4 percent) were brought into what is now the United States. Of this number, it is estimated that 40 percent came into America through South Carolina. (see CONCISE HISTORY; also BEEHIVE, BOONE HALL, BRICKMAKING, DISEASE, GULLAH, INDIGO, JONES HOTEL, LAURENS, LAZARETTO, LIBERTY HILL, MANIGAULT, OAKLAND, PEST HOUSE, PLANTATION, REMLEY'S POINT, RICE, SWEETGRASS BASKETS, TASK SYSTEM)

SNAKES – The lowcountry has the dubious distinction of being home to almost every snake indigenous to North America, both poisonous and non-poisonous. The former RICE fields and swampy lowlands are ideal habitats for a number of water snakes, including the water moccasin, also called cottonmouth for its practice of opening its mouth wide when alarmed, showing the white interior. Non-venomous black racers, rat, chicken, and king snakes are common to woods and fields. Venomous copperheads are also found here. Of the rattlesnakes, the eastern diamondback is the largest and perhaps the most prevalent. The coral snake, a member of the cobra family and ringed in black, yellow, and red, is the deadliest, but it is rare and easily confused with the non-venomous scarlet snake. Perhaps seen most commonly is the glass snake, a green snake found in yards and grassy areas—it is not a true snake but a legless lizard and completely harmless.

SNEE FARM – Primarily known as the plantation of the PINCKNEY family, Snee Farm is located on LONG POINT Road across from BOONE HALL PLANTATION. It was originally granted to Thomas Bolton, who sold it to Nathaniell Law in 1699. Some historians believe the original name was FEE FARM, so named because it came into the PINCKNEY family as payment for a legal fee. Snee Farm was a working RICE plantation when it was purchased in 1754 by Colonel Charles Pinckney. At his death in 1782, Snee Farm passed to his son Charles Pinckney (1758–1824), called "Constitution Charles" for his contributions as a delegate to the Constitutional Convention of 1787. His "Pinckney Draught" introduced 31 provisions to the constitution. Charles Pinckney's political career is one of uninterrupted and devoted service to his country. He began as the youngest man (age 22) to serve in the South Carolina House of Representatives. He was governor of South Carolina four times: in 1789, 1791, 1796, and 1806. In 1798, he served as a U.S. senator. In 1802, he was made the U.S. minister to Spain. In 1791, President George Washington stopped at Snee Farm for breakfast during his Southern Tour before making the crossing to Charleston at HIBBEN'S FERRY. While Washington breakfasted with Pinckney outside under the trees, Pinckney apologized to Washington for the informal surroundings, stating that the fare was "entirely of a farm," and that this was a place he seldom visited "or things perhaps would be in better order." Snee Farm was owned by the Hamlin family in the 19th century. The present house was built *c.* 1820, replacing an earlier house on the site. The house and grounds are now the Charles Pinckney National Historic Site, open to the public under the jurisdiction of the National Park Service. (see CONCISE HISTORY; also ALHAMBRA HALL, PINCKNEY, REVOLUTIONARY WAR, SHELL HALL, WASHINGTON)

SPANISH MOSS – Also known to early colonists as "graybeard," Spanish moss is an epiphyte, or air plant, which attaches itself to other plants (primarily trees) without harm. A bromeliad, it is a member of the pineapple family, and thrives near water and in areas of maximum sunlight and high humidity. The Indians used Spanish moss as clothing, padding for moccasins, as bedding, and in the construction of their houses. Early settlers thought moss had curative powers and placed it in shoes to relieve high blood pressure. Brewed into a tea, it was thought to help stimulate milk production after childbirth. The center core within each tendril of Spanish moss is a long, black fiber similar to horsehair. During the CIVIL WAR, this fiber was used to make rope, harnesses, and, because of the shortage of wool, woven into cavalry blankets. Until the advent of manmade fibers, it was widely used as upholstery stuffing and for padding the seats of automobiles.

SPARTINA – This tall green marsh grass (*spartina alterniflora*) both stabilizes the soft marsh mud and provides food to the salt marsh environment. A healthy salt marsh is said to produce more organic material than the most productive wheat field. When broken down by wind and waves, dead spartina mixes with other microscopic plants and plankton, creating a nutrient-rich detritus that provides the foundation of the food chain for coastal marine life. (see PLOUGH MUD)

STARVEGUT HALL – RICE plantation in CHRIST CHURCH PARISH on the WANDO RIVER and, at one point, part of WANDO PLANTATION. WILLIAM HOPTON purchased these Wando River plantations in 1759 from William VANDERHORST. One celebrated visitor to the plantation was the botanist William BARTRAM, who wrote in 1763, "set out with Mr. Hopton to his seat which he called starve gut hall on Wando River. He shewed me his rice ground & we walked in his Salt swamps." It is now part of Dunes West. (see LEXINGTON PLANTATION, VANDERHORST, WANDO PLANTATION)

STATIONS – The cross streets on SULLIVAN'S ISLAND. The name comes from the time when a trolley system traversed the island and the stops became known as "stations." (see CHARLESTON & SEASHORE RAILROAD COMPANY, COVE INLET BRIDGE, ISLE OF PALMS, OLD BRIDGE)

STATUTES – Much of the information in this work was gleaned from early laws, or statutes. Given both the archaic language of earlier times and their inherent legal nature, they often make difficult reading. One of the best examples found is the title to a 1707 statute regarding roads: "An Additional Act to a Continuing and Additional Act to an Additional Act for Making and Mending Highways, and for the Impowering the Governor for the Time Being, to Appoint Commissioners in the Rooms of Such as are Dead or Gone Off, or May Die or Go Off, and to Ascertain the Watch in Charles-Town."

STEEPLECHASE AMUSEMENT PARK – This grand amusement park was located on the front beach of ISLE OF PALMS in the late 1800s. There was a 186-foot Ferris wheel, several hotels, a large pavilion, and an ingenious steeplechase course, wherein a mechanical field of metal horses and jockeys raced a circuitous course around the pavilion to the delight of betting onlookers. (see ISLE OF PALMS)

STELLA MARIS – "Our Lady, Star of the Sea." This Catholic church on SULLIVAN'S ISLAND was erected c. 1873. The Gothic Revival building was designed by John H. Devereaux, and much of the brick used in its construction was salvaged from the ruins of FORT MOULTRIE following the CIVIL WAR. Its blue spire with St. Mary atop has long been a familiar day mark for mariners.

STRAIGHT REACH – This straight section of the original GEORGETOWN ROAD just south of the old THIRTY-TWO MILE INN near TIBWIN was once used as a racetrack. Horseracing was extremely popular in the late 18th and early 19th centuries. At one time bleachers had been erected along the side of the Straight Reach road for spectators. Only the road exists now—still unpaved and exactly 1 mile long. (see STRAWBERRY FERRY)

STRANGER'S FEVER – The general name given to a number of diseases (smallpox, influenza, yellow fever) brought into the colony by visitors (called strangers). (see DISEASE, PEST HOUSE)

STRAWBERRY CHAPEL – Formally known as St. John's Episcopal Church, Berkeley, this church was originally built as a CHAPEL OF EASE for BIGGIN Church. Erected through monies bequeathed by James Child of CHILDSBURY in 1725, this brick chapel served the parish of (lower) ST. JOHN'S PARISH, BERKELEY. After the church at Biggin burned, it became the main parish church. In 1946, communion silver that had been buried during the CIVIL WAR was discovered nearby, including a silver chalice thought to have been brought to America by a HUGUENOT émigré. Strawberry Chapel is on the National Historic Register; services are held here in the fall and the spring. (see CONCISE HISTORY; also GENERAL JAMES CHAPLIN BEECHER, CHILDSBURY, CIVIL WAR, MEPKIN, GENERAL SHERMAN, POTTER'S RAIDERS, READ, RICE HOPE)

STRAWBERRY FERRY – At CHILDSBURY, this ferry across the COOPER RIVER was first established by an act of the assembly on February 17, 1705. Here also was Strawberry Plantation. One of the most popular features of the town at Childsbury, also known as Strawberry, was horseracing, which took place on a nearby track. The "Strawberry Jockey Club" also held its regular meetings here. An advertisement in the February 11, 1766 *Gazette* announced: "To be Let. The Plantation and Ferry in St. John's Parish commonly called and known by the name of the Strawberry, whereon is a good Dwelling-house and other Out-houses, a Garden and about 80 or 100 acres of cleared Land, fit for Corn and Indigo; a Horse boat, and two Negro Men to attend the Ferry . . . There is also on said Place, a Mile Course, and a large convenient Stable with proper Stalls for Horses." (see CHILDSBURY, RICE HOPE)

SULLIVAN'S ISLAND – A BARRIER ISLAND on the eastern side of Charleston's harbor entrance. It is named for CAPTAIN FLORENCE O'SULLIVAN, who was in charge of the COASTAL WATCH and lookout and a "Great Gunn" on the island in 1674. The island's fortifications have served almost every war of the nation's history, beginning with the first Fort Sullivan (later FORT MOULTRIE) built in 1776. Beginning in the 1680s, the island served as a base for the harbor PILOTS responsible for bringing vessels safely across the bar and into Charleston harbor. The island also had the first lighthouse for Charleston until 1752, when the MORRIS ISLAND LIGHTHOUSE was erected. The present SULLIVAN'S ISLAND LIGHT was put into service in 1962. In 1707, the island was designated as an appropriate place for a quarantine station against the importation of contagious diseases, and a LAZARETTO (commonly called the PEST HOUSE) was erected at the southern point of the island. In the late 1700s, Charlestonians and EAST COOPER plantation owners began "resorting" to the island to escape the mosquito-borne illnesses of the summer months and, by 1819, when MOULTRIEVILLE was incorporated, there were 200 houses on the island. By the mid-1800s, the island had become one of the most popular resorts in America, including the showplace hotel called THE MOULTRIE HOUSE. During the CIVIL WAR, many of the homes and hotels on the island were destroyed to make way for the building of Confederate batteries or by shelling from bombardments. The Confederate submarine C.S.S. *HUNLEY* trained at BREACH INLET and it was from here that the vessel made its successful, but fateful, attack on the U.S.S. *Housatonic*. The island began to rebuild as a summering place in the 1870s and 1880s, at which time the community of ATLANTICVILLE began to grow in the mid-portion of the island. In the late 1800s and during World Wars I and II, FORT MOULTRIE was a large and active military installation and MARSHALL RESERVATION was built at the northern tip of the island overlooking BREACH INLET. The island remained primarily a summering place until the 1960s, when people began to make their permanent, year-round homes on the island. (see CONCISE HISTORY; also ATLANTIC BEACH HOTEL, DR. JOHN BACHMAN, BANDSTAND, GENERAL PIERRE BEAUREGARD, BONNET, BOWMAN'S JETTY, BREACH INLET, BRIDGE OF BOATS, CHAINY BRIAR, CHARLESTON & SEASHORE RAILROAD, CIVIL WAR, COAST GUARD STATION, COASTAL WATCH, *COMMODORE PERRY*, CROSSING THE BAR, *CYPRESS*, DISEASE, *ENTERPRISE, ETIWAN*, FLAG STREET, FRENCH/SPANISH INVASION, GOLD BUG, GRACE-CHURCH, GRILLAGE, HORNED TOADS, *HUNLEY*, I'ON, JONES HOTEL, LAZARETTO, MANHATTAN, MARSHALL RESERVATION, *COLONEL MYERS*, MYRTLE, NEW BRIGHTON HOTEL, OFFICER'S ROW, OLD BRIDGE, PLANTER'S HOTEL, *POCOSIN*, EDGAR ALLAN POE, POINT HOUSE, *PRESTO*, RAVENEL, RESORTS, *SAPPHO*, SEASIDE LABORATORY, STATIONS, STELLA MARIS, SWASH CHANNEL, TWIN TORNADOES, WILKIE'S BOARDING HOUSE)

SULLIVAN'S ISLAND LIGHT – Finished in 1962, this 163-foot tower replaced the old MORRIS ISLAND LIGHT and was originally painted in red and white. Officially known as the Charleston Light, it has the capability of being the most powerful lighthouse in the world, with a potential of 28 million candlepower. Although the COAST GUARD STATION originally manned the lighthouse, it became fully automated in 1982.

SULLIVAN'S ISLAND MAIL BOAT – From an advertisement in the July 16, 1806 *Courier*: "For the accommodation of his customers and all others who may reside on the Island, the subscriber has established a Regular Packet furnished with Sails, &c. complete; and in case of calms or squally weather, she will be furnished with four or six Oars, with good steady Oarsmen, in order to ensure a short passage. She will leave Beale's wharf every day at half past 3 o'clock in the afternoon, and return or set off from the Island every morning precisely at 6 o'clock . . . The Subscriber will be happy to see his friends at the house he occupied last year on the Island. He has a large supply of the best WINES, LIQUORS, &c. and an abundance of the best things in the eating way, and good Beds for steady customers. Jonathan Hope." (see RESORTS, SULLIVAN'S ISLAND)

SWASH CHANNEL – Also known as the Beach Channel, this channel enters the harbor between DRUNKEN DICK'S SHOALS and SULLIVAN'S ISLAND. During the CIVIL WAR, Confederate BLOCKADE RUNNERS used this channel for the protection it provided due to its proximity to the guns of FORT MOULTRIE. Doing so was tricky; there were the hazards of the shoals and the rocks at the GRILLAGE on Sullivan's Island. Many ships went aground in the attempt.(see C.S.S. *CELT, PRESTO*)

SWEETGRASS BASKETS/BASKET STANDS – The two areas in the world where the distinctively coiled SWEETGRASS BASKETS are sewn (not woven) are Sierra Leone and the Carolina lowcountry. Using a technique brought by African slaves to the RICE plantations and handed down from generation to generation, the baskets were originally used for utilitarian purposes. The "fanna" basket, a large, flat, circular basket made from local grasses, was used to winnow rice (the grain separated from the chaff by a process called "fanning") and to toss the rice high into the air (a method still used in Sierra Leone). The baskets now sold on Highway 17 roadside stands and in Charleston's city market are decorative "show" baskets. Their uniqueness, artistry, and place in African-American history have gained worldwide attention. Baskets sewn by MOUNT PLEASANT families are part of permanent collections at the Smithsonian Institute and The American Museum of Natural History as well as other museums. (see MANIGAULT, RICE, SLAVERY)

TABBY – A mortar made of lime, crushed oyster shell, and water. Much of the earliest European construction in the lowcountry was built with tabby. Spanish explorers in the 1520s described visiting an Indian village with buildings that had the walls made of "a mortar which they make of oyster shells." The word is derived from the Spanish *tabi*. (see OYSTER)

TASK SYSTEM – Work for field hands on most lowcountry plantations was through a method called the task system. Each day a hand was given a task to perform by the "captain" or "boss" (usually a slave with leadership abilities) who divided the tasks, knowing from personal experience how long it would take a specific individual to complete his or her task. Tasks (a quarter, half, or full acre) were then divided according to age, sex, and ability. Tasks were usually complete by mid-afternoon when field work would halt and a meal would be served. This is the origin of the uniquely Charleston custom of having a "three o'clock dinner" as the main meal of the day. (see PLANTATIONS, SLAVERY)

TEE, THE – The name given to the area where the COOPER RIVER splits into two branches (the EAST BRANCH and WEST BRANCH), forming a tee. The plantation settled here by the Coming family in the late 1600s was called COMINGTEE.

TEN-MILE HOUSE – Colloquially known as Mulatto Tavern, this was one of the stops along the GEORGETOWN ROAD between the HOBCAW FERRY and the SANTEE RIVER. Historian Petrona McIver wrote that "belated passengers from Georgetown, too late to catch the ferries, stopped overnight here; and local travelers going to a distant plantation sometimes used it to make a break in the trip. No hint of the exact location of this house has been discovered, but ten miles from Mount Pleasant would locate it near Elm Grove and Whitehall Plantations." (see INNS & TAVERNS)

THIRTY-TWO MILE INN – This was the most commodious of the inns along the GEORGETOWN ROAD, so named since it was 32 miles from the HOBCAW FERRY. Located south of McCLELLANVILLE and just west of TIBWIN, this pre-Revolutionary War inn was a main stop for travelers and provided accommodations for overnight stay. Described as a large, English-style hostelry, it had stables and a dining hall. Horse races were held on the nearby 1-mile track called STRAIGHT REACH. It was also at one point called JONES TAVERN. It was torn down in the 1950s. (see INNS & TAVERNS, STRAIGHT REACH)

THOMAS ISLAND – An island adjoining DANIEL ISLAND to the northwest. On May 10, 1673, 270 acres were surveyed for William Thomas, a gentleman who arrived from Northumberland County, Virginia, with his wife, Mary, daughter, indentured servants, and slaves. Thomas received additional land grants in ensuing years, and, for a time during the earliest years of settlement, Daniel Island was referred to as "Mr. Thomas's Island." Other land grants followed and, by 1685, a colonist wrote, "Thomas Island all taken up." (see CONCISE HISTORY; also CLEMENT'S FERRY ROAD, CLOUTER CREEK, GROVE PLANTATION, COOPER RIVER, LOGAN, MAWAN)

TIBWIN – Just south of McCLELLANVILLE, this small rural community near the THIRTY-TWO MILE INN takes its name from Tibwin Plantation, established c. 1705 by John Collins. In his will, dated 1707, Collins leaves his son Alexander his "Tebwin" plantation. At times, Tibwin has been owned by the VANDERHORST, Mathews, Morrison, Skipper, and Leland families. Almost destroyed by the hurricane of 1822, the two-story house, originally built overlooking BULL'S BAY, was moved farther inland, rolled on logs to its present position, and rebuilt. Tibwin was a RICE plantation and the diked ponds are still extant. The name is undoubtedly of Native American origin, meaning unknown. (see AWENDAW, BULL'S ISLAND, COLLINS CREEK, JONES TAVERN, LAUREL HILL, MATHEW'S FERRY, STRAIGHT REACH, THIRTY-TWO MILE INN, WASHASHAW)

TIMICAU – The Native American name (meaning unknown) for DEWEES ISLAND. In 1714, John and Mary Gwin sold 8,110 acres "being on an island . . . commonly called Timicau." This was one of the HUNTING ISLANDS of the SEWEE. (see BARRIER ISLAND)

TIPPYCUTLAW – Also variously spelled as *Tibbekudlaw*, *Tibicop Haw*, and *Tippycop Law*, the Native American for the hill upon which BIGGIN Church was built. In 1712, John COLLETON gave 3 acres for a church to be built "upon Tibicop Haw Hill" in WADBOO Barony. Tipicad Daw House was a name given to the Colleton plantation. Later owned by Philip PORCHER, it became known as Tiverton Lawn. (see BIGGIN, WADBOO)

TOOMER'S BRICKYARD – Now part of Dunes West, this plantation in CHRIST CHURCH PARISH had a BRICKYARD on Toomer Creek, a tributary on the east side of the WANDO RIVER. Henry Toomer (d. 1739) came to Carolina from England; his son Joshua (1712–1763) married Mary Bonneau, daughter of Huguenot émigré Antoine Bonneau. Their son, Joshua Bonneau Toomer (1740–1796), married Mary Sabina VANDERHORST, and both are buried at WAPPETAW. Their son, Dr. Anthony Vanderhorst Toomer (1775–1856), was a prominent planter and physician who served as a captain in the War of 1812. (see BRICKMAKING, LAUREL HILL, LEXINGTON PLANTATION, WAPPETAW)

TOOTHACHE TREE – Also known as sea ash, prickly ash, or Hercules Club, commonly found on BARRIER ISLANDS. The bark and leaves of the toothache tree (*Zanthoxylum americanum*) were once used medicinally for the Novocain-like numbing substance they contain. Placed on the gums, it could ease a toothache. The trunks and limbs of this indigenous woody shrub are covered with sharp, claw-shaped barbs.

TOTE – A GULLAH term meaning "to carry." The word is derived from the African word *tote*, meaning "to lift a load from one's head without help."

TURTLES – In 1681, colonist Thomas Ashe wrote, "in Carolina there are the Turtle of three sorts – the Hawk's Bill . . . the Green Turtle . . . the Loggerhead . . . they are a sort of creatures which live both on land & water . . . In the night they often come ashore to lay their eggs in the sand . . . which in due time produces her young ones." Female loggerheads still make their way up BARRIER ISLAND beaches to lay their eggs in the summer months. Because their population has dwindled drastically for various environmental and man-driven reasons, the loggerhead turtle is now on the endangered species list. Their nests are fiercely protected by turtle "patrols" who walk area beaches each morning in the summer months to look for new nests. When found, the nest (a funnel-shaped hole buried in the sand) is then carefully dug, with each round, leathery egg carefully removed and placed in a bucket in the exact upright position as it laid in the nest. After the eggs are counted, they are then carefully reburied in the nest, which is then marked off with tape. Hatchlings, which usually dig out at night, find their way to the sea by following the light on the water made by either the moon or stars. This is why households on beachfronts are asked to shield their exterior lights; otherwise the baby turtles can become confused and crawl towards land instead of the sea. Of the hundred or so eggs laid, only a handful will live to maturity. (see COOTER)

TWENTY-ONE MILE – The ELBOW TAVERN was for many years a mustering place for the local militia. This tavern on the old Georgetown Road was located 21 miles from the ferry at HOBCAW. (see GEORGETOWN ROAD, INNS & TAVERNS)

TWIN TORNADOES – On May 4, 1761, a remarkable phenomenon occurred when two separate waterspouts, one beginning on the upper reaches of the COOPER RIVER and the other developing up the ASHLEY RIVER near Wappoo Creek, came down each river almost simultaneously, eventually joining at REBELLION ROAD to form one powerful waterspout. Forty vessels were anchored there at the time and, according to a report in the *Gazette*, the first waterspout "laid every vessel in its course on their beam-ends . . . and many with the ends of their top-sail yards in the water, sinking one ship, three snows, and a sloop outright." The second one "instantaneously set them upright again as they lay on their sides, the whole being over in less than two minutes." The joined waterspouts then roared over SULLIVAN'S ISLAND and out to sea. Only four lives were lost in this unusual occurrence.

VANDERHORST – Pronounced *Van-dross*. Captain John Vanderhorst (d. 1739) purchased the property known as LEXINGTON PLANTATION on the upper WANDO RIVER in 1712. His son, REVOLUTIONARY WAR hero Major John Vanderhorst (1718–1787), served as South Carolina secretary of state. Arnoldus Vanderhorst (1748–1815) was a delegate to the Provincial Congress in 1775 and 1776, was twice mayor of Charleston, and was governor of South Carolina from 1792 to 1794. He also had a plantation on KIAWAH Island, and the Vanderhorst mansion there still retains his name. (see STARVEGUT HALL, TIBWIN, WAPPETAW)

VENNING – Both Venning Street in the OLD VILLAGE area of MOUNT PLEASANT and Venning Road (also known as FOUR-MILE ROAD) are named for the Venning family. This family, long associated with CHRIST CHURCH PARISH, may have arrived with the New England DISSENTERS who settled at WAPPETAW in 1697. Samuel Venning (d. 1821) was a REVOLUTIONARY WAR patriot who gained notoriety at the BATTLE OF VIDEAU BRIDGE, where he shot British captain "Mad" Archie Campbell. The main Venning plantation was MYRTLE GROVE. The Venning family genealogy runs like a who's who of early CHRIST CHURCH PARISH families. Samuel Venning (1797–1840) married Ann Lucas, daughter of JONATHAN LUCAS. Their daughter, Anne Lucas, married Ferdinand GREGORIE (1819–1880), and their son, Ferdinand II, married Anne Palmer PORCHER, daughter of Philip Edward Porcher and Elizabeth Catherine Palmer. Nicholas Venning (1745–1835) owned BELVUE-BERMUDA plantation. (see BERMUDA TOWN, BRABANT, CIVIL WAR, LAUREL HILL, LIBERTY HILL, PALMETTO GROVE, BATTLE OF VIDEAU BRIDGE, WAPPETAW)

VIDEAU BRIDGE, BATTLE OF – One of the last skirmishes of the REVOLUTIONARY WAR, this engagement occurred on January 3, 1782, near the bridge crossing FRENCH QUARTER CREEK on the Cooper River's EAST BRANCH. The bridge takes its name from the Videau family. In 1700, French

HUGUENOT Peter Videau had a grant for 200 acres in the "Parish of St. Denis or Orange Quarter." (see ORANGE QUARTER)

VILLAGE, THE – Local name for the old town of MOUNT PLEASANT. Likewise, the town of McCLELLANVILLE is called "the village" by locals. (see GREENWICH VILLAGE, HIBBEN'S FERRY, HILLIARDSVILLE, MOUNT PLEASANT PLANTATION, OLD VILLAGE)

VILLEPONTOUX – The Carolina patriarchs of this HUGUENOT family were Pierre Villepontoux and his son, Zachariah (1698–1780), who first emigrated to New Rochelle, New York, before coming to CAROLINA. On Parnassus Plantation on the Back River near Goose Creek, Zachariah established one of the largest BRICKMAKING concerns in the region. He both designed and furnished the bricks for POMPION HILL Chapel. His brother, Peter, had a plantation and LIME KILN at SHEM CREEK. Following Peter's death in 1748, the *Gazette* of October 30, 1752, describes his Shem Creek land as "containing 430 acres of land, joining the plantation of Jacob Motte, Esq. and is on a navigable river; here is a great quantity of oak and yellow pine lying on the ground which is blown down by the late hurricane, and will serve for sewing of boards, etc. It is a convenient place for the making of lime, and about 3 miles from Charleston." The name is now usually spelled *Villeponteaux*. (see BRICKMAKING, LIME KILN, POMPION HILL, SHEM CREEK)

WACCAMAW – A river flowing into WINYAH BAY near Georgetown. The name is of Indian origin, possibly the place FRANCISCO OF CHICORA described as "the land of Guacaya." The Waccamaw River was a center for some of the finest RICE plantations in the country during the 18th and 19th centuries.

WADBOO – Also variously spelled *Watboo, Watbooe, Watbu, Watt-boo-e, Woodboo*. The name of this creek and swamp between the headwaters of the Cooper River's WEST BRANCH to BIGGIN Creek is undoubtedly of Native American origin, meaning unknown except that the "-boo" at the end of a word likely refers to a body of water. Wadboo Barony was granted in 1690 to Landgrave James COLLETON, the third son of Sir John Colleton, and Wadboo Plantation was his country seat. In 1699, Peter Girard was granted 350 acres near "Watboe Plantation"; Henry Noble had a grant in 1704 "on Watboo." In 1706, Anthony Cordes had a warrant for land "Joyning to Watboo line." In 1769, Stephen Mazyck's will mentions "the plantation where I now live purchased of Messrs. Paul, Isaac and Benjamin Trapier in Biggin Swamp called Grand Fountain or Wootboo." BIGGIN Church is about 2 miles west of the Wadboo Bridge. On August 29, 1782, the Americans met the British at the Battle of Wadboo Plantation. Wrote FRANCIS MARION a day later, "Major Frazier with a hundred horse & some Coloured Dragoons, came on in full charge, I let them come within thirty yards and threw in a fire from my left which was advanced under the cover of three small houses; the fire was so well directed that the Enemy immediately broke and Retreated in Confusion . . . " (see BARONY, REVOLUTIONARY WAR, TIPPYCUTLAW, WISKINBOO)

WADING PLACE – Shown on early 18th-century maps of DANIEL ISLAND, this was presumably a low area on the road that led to the ferry where a creek or rivulet required fording. A 1712 statute requiring residents to keep the road in repair referred to a bridge " . . . over the Creek on the NW side of Thomas Island commonly called the Wading Place." Its general location today is on CLEMENTS FERRY ROAD in the lowland area just before the Mark Clark Expressway. (see THOMAS ISLAND)

WADMACON – Also variously spelled as *Wadbacan*, *Wattohan*, and *Watahan*, it is the Native American name for an island area on the South SANTEE RIVER near FRENCH SANTEE. In 1698, Major John Boone had a warrant for 500 acres on land "where the Sewee Indians lived upon Same called by the Indians Mockand." While it has been thought that this was the original land grant for BOONE HALL, it is likely that "Mockand" was instead a variant of "Wadmacon," since his son, Thomas Boone, later inherited the land at "Wadbacan Island " on the Santee. Other early grantees of the area included Daniel HUGER (*c.* 1696) and Elias Horry of HAMPTON PLANTATION. (see BOONE HALL)

WAKENDAW – Also variously spelled as *Wackendaw* and *Wacanoaw*, the name is of Native American origin, meaning unknown. In 1695, Nathaniell Law received a grant for 200 acres "upon wackingdaw Creek . . . formlery possessed by Dinis Morr . . . Coll Godfrey & Rich Searell but there was noe grant for the same." In 1697, David Maybank's warrant for 200 acres at HOBCAW was adjoining "Wackendawe Creeke." This area on the northern side of HOBCAW was later the site of LYNCH'S GROVE Plantation. Wakendaw Creek was at times called Cornbow (or COINBOW) and also QUELCH'S CREEK. (see CONCISE HISTORY; also HOPSEWEE, MOLASSES CREEK, QUELCH'S CREEK)

WAMBAW – Also variously spelled as *Wamba*, this creek is a tributary of the South SANTEE RIVER in the region known as FRENCH SANTEE. It flows through what is known as Big and Little Wambaw Swamp. French HUGUENOT émigré Daniel HUGER was granted land on "Wambah" Creek adjoining lands of Peter de St. Julien and Paul Mazyck. In 1723, Elias Horry purchased 1,000 acres "on Wamba Cricke." The name is undoubtedly of Indian origin, meaning unknown. The area, now dense swamp, was once cleared for RICE cultivation. The June 20–27, 1760 *Gazette* announced: "To be sold at publick Vendue . . . The plantation known by the name of WAMBAW, containing 500 acres, 200 of which is good river swamp, belonging to Tacitus Gaillard, Esq.; situated on Santee river in St. James' parish, on which is as very good dwelling house and sundry convenient out-houses." (see FRENCH SANTEE, HAMPTON PLANTATION, ST. JAMES SANTEE)

WAMPANCHECOONE – Also spelled *Wampacheroone*, this was the Native American name for Horlbeck Creek. It is first mentioned in a grant in 1679 to Anthony Shorey for 200 acres "on Wampacheroone Creek." In 1681, Theophilus Patey received a grant for 470 acres on "creeke called Wawpachecoone." The will of Thomas Boone mentions "land where I now live . . . on Wapeckecoon Creek." The name changed to Horlbeck when John and Peter Horlbeck owned BOONE HALL. (see BRICKMAKING, BRICKYARD PLANTATION)

WANDO – A coastal Indian tribe who lived along the WANDO RIVER. Like the ETIWAN, they may have been part of the KIAWAH tribe. The name is a possible variation of the Muskhogean word for deer and at times is spelled as *Wantoot*. It is thought that this small tribe was completely eradicated by an epidemic of smallpox in 1698. Affra Coming, the wife of John Coming of COMINGTEE, wrote, "The small pox . . . has been mortal to all sorts of the inhabitants & especially the Indians who tis said to have swept away a whole neighboring nation, all to 5 or 6 which ran away and left their dead unburied, lying on the ground for the vultures to devour." She was likely speaking of the Wando. (see DISEASE)

WANDO PLANTATION – Now comprising most of Dunes West, on the east side of the WANDO RIVER, across from CAINHOY. This RICE, LUMBER, and BRICKMAKING plantation began as separate tracts owned by the LOGAN family and in 1743, by physician LIONEL CHALMERS, whose wife was Martha Logan. The properties were combined in 1759 under the ownership of Charleston merchant WILLIAM HOPTON and included the plantations known as STARVEGUT HALL and LEXINGTON PLANTATION. Owners in the 19th century included the GREGORIE family and Dr. John O'Hear. In the 1940s, this was the country estate of the Princess Henrietta Hartford Pignatelli, the wife of Prince Guido Pignatelli de Montecaivo of Rome. (see BARTRAM, CAINHOY FERRY, LEXINGTON PLANTATION, O'HEAR'S POINT, WEEHOY)

WANDO RIVER – This river is unusual in that it runs parallel to the coastline, with its headwaters originating in swampland approximately 20 miles north of MOUNT PLEASANT above WAPPETAW. The river flows southward into Charleston harbor. The original designation for most of the area east of the Cooper River was Wando Neck. PLANTATIONS were established along both shores of the Wando River soon after the settlement of CHARLES TOWN; they were largely given to RICE and BRICKMAKING. The river served as the main "roadway" between plantation and town; the ferry at CAINHOY was the transportation hub. (see CONCISE HISTORY; also ABOVE THE SALTS, BRICKMAKING, CAINHOY, CAT ISLAND, DATA, GUERIN'S BRIDGE, HOG ISLAND CHANNEL, PLANTATIONS, RICE)

WAPPETAW – The Native American word for the area on the eastern shore of the headwaters of the WANDO RIVER near FIFTEEN-MILE ROAD. The lands in this region were first granted to George Smith (son of Landgrave Thomas Smith) in 1697. The Wappetaw Landing area was owned by BENJAMIN QUELCH and, later, Richard Capers. At times referred to as the SEWEE Settlement, in 1696–97, this area was settled by 52 Congregationalist DISSENTERS from Ipswich, Massachusetts. The exact family names of this group are not known, but it is thought the Hartman, Hollybush, Murrell, Oliver, Severance, DORRELL, VANDERHORST, VENNING, Toomer, White, and WHILDEN families were part of their number. Either part of this group or a separate group from New England may have also been the families who settled at CAINHOY and established the meeting house there. (see CONCISE HISTORY; also ANDERSONVILLE, DEARSLEY, FENWICK, GUERIN'S BRIDGE, INNS & TAVERNS, LAUREL HILL, SIXTEEN-MILE HOUSE, WAPPETAW MEETING HOUSE)

WAPPETAW MEETING HOUSE – Also known as Old Wappetaw. It was established in around 1699 by the New England Congregationalists for the Sewee Settlement. The Wappetaw Meeting was usually served by the same minister who had charge of the CAINHOY MEETING HOUSE. During the REVOLUTIONARY WAR, the church was used as barracks by British troops under Sir Banestre Tarleton; the British burned the church in 1782. A second church was rebuilt in 1786, also known as the Independent Church in CHRIST CHURCH PARISH. During the CIVIL WAR, Union troops used the pews and interior woodwork for firewood. The church was never rebuilt, and, in 1867, the congregation joined with the Charleston Presbytery. In 1872, a new church was built in McCLELLANVILLE called New Wappetaw Presbyterian Church. In 1897, the old Wappetaw Church collapsed in ruins. Only the burial ground remains. Gravestones include members of the Anderson, Capers, Hamlin, Morrison, Toomer, VANDERHORST, White, and Whiteside families, among others. (see CONCISE HISTORY; also ANDERSONVILLE, CAINHOY MEETING HOUSE, DISSENTERS, ROBERT FENWICK, LAUREL HILL)

WASHASHAW – Native American word for the creek flowing into the South SANTEE RIVER just above McCLELLANVILLE, now known as COLLINS CREEK. The spelling of the word has changed erratically depending on the writer, shown variously as *Waha*, *Washaw*, *Washo*, and *Waslishoe*. (see HOPSEWEE, TIBWIN, WASHO)

WASHINGTON'S SOUTHERN TOUR – In May 1791, President George Washington visited Charleston on his grand tour through the Southern states. After crossing the SANTEE RIVER, he first stopped at HAMPTON PLANTATION, where he was entertained by ELIZA LUCAS PINCKNEY and her daughter, Harriott Pinckney Horry. He next stayed the night at Joseph MANIGAULT's plantation at AWENDAW, and then breakfasted with Charles PINCKNEY at SNEE FARM. Arriving at HIBBEN FERRY, he was rowed across the harbor to Charleston in a special barge provided by Major Peter Bocquet, which had been lengthened at Pritchard's Shipyard at HOBCAW for the occasion. Twelve masters of American vessels manned the oars, escorted by a flotilla of boats of all sizes, which were filled with people and musical bands. (see SALT HOPE, SEWEE BARONY)

WASHO – A variant of WASHASHAW, the Native American designation for the area and creek along the South SANTEE RIVER just above McCLELLANVILLE. JONATHAN LUCAS erected his second RICE mill at Washo Plantation for General Thomas PINCKNEY. (see RICE)

WATCOW, WATTICOE – Variant spellings of WATROO, the Native American name for the easternmost portion of BERESFORD CREEK on DANIEL ISLAND. In 1680, James Hutton of "Ittiwan Island" sold Philip Doldridge his plantation on "Watcow Creek." In 1681, Edmund and Hannah FOGARTIE owned 250 acres "being upon a certain parcill of land inhabited by Indians and known by the name of Watcow." In 1765, Charleston furniture maker Thomas Elfe purchased 65 acres from Benjamin Burnham "on Watticoe Creek." (see BERESFORD CREEK, DANIEL ISLAND)

WATROO – Variant spelling of WATCOW, the easternmost portion of BERESFORD CREEK.

WATSON'S FERRY – Name of the HOBCAW Ferry. An act in 1733 established the ferry "at the Plantation of Mr. William Watson, commonly called Hobcaw, to Charleston."

WATTESAW – Native American name (meaning unknown) for the area just north of the FRENCH QUARTER on the Cooper River's EAST BRANCH, now BLESSING plantation. In 1682, Jonah Lynch was granted 780 acres "at a place called Wattesaw also the Blessing." (see THE BLESSING, EAST BRANCH, POYAS)

WEEHOY – Native American place name (meaning unknown) for the area on the WANDO RIVER on the north side of the west branch of Horlbeck Creek. It is first mentioned in 1694, when ROBERT FENWICK is granted 500 acres on Wando River "knowne by ye name Data" and adjoining "Major Boon's land on the one side, and to a place named Weehoy on the other side." In 1697, Nathaniel Snow had a warrant for the land lying between "Dauhe and Weeho Plantations." In 1720, the will of George LOGAN of WANDO PLANTATION mentions his plantation called Wehoe (also spelled in the will as *Weeahoe*), where his son George lives. (see DATA, ROBERT FENWICK, LEXINGTON PLANTATION)

WEST BRANCH, COOPER RIVER – The COOPER RIVER divides into two distinct branches approximately 20 miles inland: the EAST BRANCH and the

West Branch. The West Branch continues inland to WADBOO near MONCKS CORNER. Like the East Branch, this river became a major RICE-producing area. John IRVING described the river in the 1840s: "After passing Strawberry Ferry, there is on both sides of the river one unbroken extent of cultivation, a sea of waving green to the head of the river." Plantations on the eastern shore of the West Branch included STRAWBERRY, Clermont, Elwood, MEPKIN, Washington, Glebe, Buck Hall, Pawley, South Chachan, North Chachan, Willlow Grove, Umbria, and Sportsman Retreat. (see CHILDSBURY, DR. BENJAMIN READ, RICE HOPE)

WHILDEN – The first of this family (long associated with CHRIST CHURCH PARISH) to come to CAROLINA was likely John Whilden, born *c.* 1664 in Yarmouth, Massachusetts. It is thought that he was one of the Congregationalists who settled at WAPPETAW in the 1690s. His son, Jonathan (d. 1736), married Elizabeth DuBose, daughter of French HUGUENOT émigré Isaac DuBose of FRENCH SANTEE. During the CIVIL WAR, Charles E. Whilden was with Maxcy Gregg's First Regiment, South Carolina Volunteers. Louis Augustus Whilden was captain of the ST. JAMES MOUNTED RIFLEMEN. Whildren Street in Mount Pleasant's OLD VILLAGE takes its name from this family. (see CIVIL WAR, DISSENTERS, LAUREL HILL, WAPPETAW)

WHIPPOORWILL – JOHN LAWSON wrote that the whippoorwill was "so named because it makes those words exactly." A member of the nightjar family, the whippoorwill (*Caprimulgus vociferous*) generally sleeps in leafy underbrush by day and forages at night for flying insects. According to an Indian legend, these birds represented the departed spirits of those slain in massacre. Early colonists thought it an ill omen if one began to call near a house or a dwelling, for it meant that someone in the family would soon die.

WHITEHALL – A community overlooking COPAHEE SOUND, approximately 10 miles north of MOUNT PLEASANT. The name is derived from Whitehall Plantation, established by John White, *c.* 1715.

WILD DUNES – This private resort on the northern end of ISLE OF PALMS was first developed in the 1970s. Dunes West now incorporates most of WANDO PLANTATION. (see ISLE OF PALMS, LEXINGTON PLANTATION, WANDO PLANTATION)

WILKIE'S BOARDING HOUSE – Mrs. Wilkie kept a private boarding house on the front beach of Sullivan's Island at MOULTRIEVILLE, *c.* 1839.

WINYAH BAY – At GEORGETOWN, this bay takes it name from an Indian word possibly meaning "meat" or "deer." Winyah may also be the Yen-Yohol people mentioned in the list of tribes given to Spanish historian Peter Martyr by FRANCISCO OF CHICORA in 1521. (see FRANCISCO OF CHICORA)

WISBOO – Native American name for FRENCH QUARTER CREEK, meaning unknown, although the "-boo" at the end of the word usually denotes a place near a watercourse. In 1708, a William Sherman had a warrant for land "fronting on Cooper River & whisboo Creeck." Also spelled variously as *Whisboo*, *Wistobo*, and *Wiskbo*.

WISKINBOO – Native American name for a place and a creek in WADBOO swamp, meaning unknown. Wiskinboo Barony was granted to Landgrave Thomas Smith in 1717. In 1748, the will of Thomas Cordes mentions his "plantation called Whiskinboo." Also variously spelled as *Whiskingboo* and *Whiskenboo*. (see BARONY)

WOOD STORK – Also called wood ibis, the wood stork (*Mycteria americana*) is the only true stork native to America. Early-18th-century naturalist MARK CATESBY called the bird the "Wood Pelican," describing the bird as having a bill "nine inches and a half long, and curved towards the end; and next the head very big." Wood storks feed in marsh flat shallows and nest in nearby trees. Wrote Catesby, "They sit in great numbers on tall cypress and other trees, in an erect posture, resting their ponderous bills on their necks for their greater ease."

XOYE – Name given to the SEWEE by the Spanish in the 1500s.

YADHAW – Native American name (meaning unknown) for the area on the Cooper River's EAST BRANCH near QUINBY. It was mentioned in a 1681 grant to John Ashby for 2,000 acres "at a place called by the Indians Yadhaw." (see QUINBY)

YAM – The common word for sweet potato. The word originates with the African word *yambi*, which means "to eat." (see GULLAH)

YAUPON – Also called CASSINA, a tree indigenous to the coast and a member of the holly family. The name is from *ya-pa*, the Native American word for this shrub. The land just to the north of the ISLE OF PALMS connector on RIFLE RANGE ROAD was once Yaupon Plantation. (see BLACK DRINK, CASSINA)

YOUGHALL PLANTATION – This plantation in CHRIST CHURCH PARISH near PORCHER'S BLUFF was purchased by Abraham MOTTE for the Perrie family in 1704, set between the Hamlin lands and OAKLAND PLANTATION on the MOUNT PLEASANT seacoast. The name came from the Perrie's home of Youghall, Ireland. Youghall Road is located just south of PORCHER'S BLUFF Road, off Highway 17 North. First granted to Captain George Dearsley in 1696, portions of the property were afterwards owned by William Capers, Thomas Hamlin, George Benison (who was married to Elizabeth Capers), and eventually, in the 1850s, by the PORCHER family. (see OAKLAND PLANTATION)

YUCCA – Also known as Spanish bayonet. The long, spiked leaves of the yucca have an extremely sharp point containing a mild poison. Indigenous to the coastal area, it blooms with a long center panicle of delicate white blossoms.

ZANTEE – Alternative spelling for SANTEE, which was an Indian tribe who lived on the SANTEE RIVER from the coast to where the present-day town of Santee is located. The name perhaps means "river."

Hurricane Alley
1686-1993

THE NICKNAME HURRICANE ALLEY, GIVEN to the coastline between Cape Hatteras and lower South Carolina, was well earned. Since 1670, there have been well over 100 tropical storms or hurricanes to scream through Hurricane Alley, over one-fourth of which have been severe, Hugo-sized storms. There have even been some years when two or more storms called upon the Carolina coastline. Although meteorologists did not begin naming hurricanes until the early 1950s, detailed records were kept of storms from the very beginnings of the colony, and severe blows were remembered for the year in which they occurred, such as The Great Gale of 1804.

1686 – September 4 – This heavy gale struck with sudden fury, and was called the Spanish Repulse Hurricane since it drove away a Spanish fleet from St. Augustine preparing to attack Charles Town.

1700 – September 14 – This major hurricane had a storm surge reported as "very severe, overthrowing many houses and overflowing the town." This is the hurricane that caused the Scottish ship *Rising Sun* to break up, killing all on board.

1713 – September 15 – Seventy people were killed, with damage to shipping, houses, plantations, and fortifications.

1722 – September 19

1724 – August 28

1728 – August 13 – Charleston overflowed, with serious damage to buildings, wharves, and rice fields outside town; 23 ships were sunk or driven ashore.

1752 – September 15 – "the FLOOD came in like a bore, filling the harbor in a few minutes," wrote the *Gazette* of this extremely severe storm and its 17-foot storm surge, which swept the Pest House on Sullivan's Island to Hobcaw Point, with 14 people inside.

1752 – September 30 – Landfall near Edisto.

1753 – September 15

1758 – August 23

1761 – June 1

1769 – September 28

1770 – June 6

1778 – August 10

1781 – August 10 – Two British ships sank in the harbor.

1783 – October 7 – This hurricane washed away the original Fort Moultrie.

1784 – September 10 – Severe; 500 people drowned.

1787 – September 19 – Severe; 23 people drowned.

1792 – October 30

1797 – October 19 – Major storm, extremely high tides.

1800 – October 4 – Major storm; washing away houses on Sullivan's Island.

1804 – September 7 – The Great Gale of 1804; 500 deaths, Sullivan's Island under water. The *Courier* wrote of a ship wrecked off Cape Romain and how a Mr. Groves, with "a seaman by the name of Wallace, CAUGHT HOLD OF A HEN COOP, the OTHER PERSONS on board . . . WENT DOWN WITH THE VESSEL. Wallace kept his hold on the hen coop about four hours, when EXHAUSTED, he fell off and DROWNED." Groves was saved 12 hours later. This storm all but destroyed Fort Moultrie.

1806 – August 22 – Hits north of Charleston and ruins the cotton crop.

1806 – October 8

1810 – September 11

1811 – September 10 – A minimal storm, but with high casualties.

1813 – August 27 – The *Courier* writes of the most "TREMENDOUS GALE: In the morning THE ISLAND exhibited a MOST MELANCHOLY PICTURE, fragments of houses, furniture, boats, etc. were thrown promiscuously over it, and the BODIES OF NINE PERSONS, four of them females, lay among the ruins, an awful remembrance of THE HORRORS . . . It is supposed that as many as FIFTEEN HAVE PERISHED."

1814 – July 1 – Spawned deadly tornadoes.

1815 – September 2

1817 – August 7

1820 – September 10 – The Great Winyah Hurricane; destroyed
        Georgetown rice crops.

1822 – September 27 – Severe; washed 25 ships ashore on Sullivan's
        Island; 200 drowned.

1825 – June 3

1827 – August 25

1830 – August 13 – The Atlantic Coast Hurricane of 1830; destroyed rice
        crops.

1834 – September 4

1835 – September 18

1837 – August 16 – Offshore hurricane with heavy shipping losses.

1837 – September 1

1837 – October 8

1839 – August 28 – The Atlantic Coast Hurricane of 1839.

1841 – August 23 – Two feet of water on Market Street.

1842 – July 12

1842 – October 4

1844 – September 9

1846 – August 16

1846 – October 10

1850 – August 24

1851 – August 24 – Minor storm; came overland from Florida.

1852 – August 27 – Minor storm; came overland from Mobile, Alabama.

1854 – September 7 – The Great Gale of 1854; Sullivan's Island
        submerged. One writer described the scene on the island: "the
        homes all over the island went down like card-houses; ere long the
        Moultrie House was the only building left standing . . . There was
        one spot of greater safety, the Fort."

1856 – August 31 – Hit northern coast; extreme tides.

1871 – August 19

1872 – October 25

1874 – September 23

1876 – September 15

1877 – October 3

1878 – September 11 – Minor; affected both Carolinas.

1878 – October 22 – Major; severe damage in North Carolina.

1881 – August 27 – Severe lower coast storm; destroyed Edingsville Island
        near Edisto; more than 700 people killed.

1882 – October 11

1883 – September 11 – Major storm; severe damage to rice crops.

1885 – August 25 – The Great August Cyclone; an extreme storm; 21
        killed in South Carolina.

1886 – July 1

1887 – August 20

1889 – September 23

1893 – August 23 – Surge is 6 to 8 feet high over East Battery, with "thick spray . . . beating over the housetops."

1893 – August 27 – "The West Indian Cyclone"; an extreme storm; from 1,000 to 2,000 killed in South Carolina.

1893 – October 13 – Major storm; 22 killed in North Carolina.

1893 – October 22 – Minor storm; just south of Cape Hatteras.

1894 – September 27

1896 – September 29

1898 – October 2 – Extreme on lower coast and Georgia; 179 killed in Georgia.

1899 – October 31 – Major; extremely high tidal surge.

1904 – September 14

1906 – September 15 – Major; came in at Myrtle Beach.

1906 – October 25 – Center remained offshore.

1908 – October 9

1908 – October 22

1910 – October 19

1911 – August 27   Major storm; 17 killed in Charleston.

1912 – July 14 – Minimal; center near Savannah.

1913 – October 8 – Minimal; came in at Georgetown.

1914 – September 17

1916 – July 14 – Made landfall at Bull's Bay.

1921 – October 26

1924 – September 16

1924 – September 29

1926 – July 28

1927 – October 2

1928 – August 10

1928 – September 18 – Severe; damaged construction of the Cooper River Bridge; Folly Beach lost 15 feet of beach; $3–$5 million in losses; 5 killed.

1929 – October 1

1933 – September 6 – Brought 10.33 inches of rain.

1934 – May 28

1935 – September 5 – This hurricane destroyed the Florida Keys.

1940 – August 11 – Severe; $6.6 million in damage; $3.3 million in crop losses; 13-foot storm surge; 34 people killed.

1944 – October 20

1945 – June 24 – Severe; $6–$7 million in damages.

1945 – September 17

1946 – October 8

1947 – October 15

1949 – August 28
1950 – October 17
1950 – October 25
1952 – August 31 – ABEL; minimal.
1954 – October 15 – HAZEL; extreme; landfall at Myrtle Beach; 20
     killed.
1955 – August 16 – DIANE; minimal.
1956 – September 25 – FLOSSY
1959 – July 9 – CINDY
1959 – September 29 – GRACIE; severe; center at Edisto.
1960 – July 29 – BRENDA
1960 – September 11 – DONNA
1963 – October 25 – GINNY
1964 – August 29 – CLEO
1964 – September 12 – DORA
1966 – June 10 – ALMA
1968 – June 7 – ABBY
1968 – October 19 – GLADYS
1979 – September 4 – DAVID
1989 – September 21 – HUGO; extreme; center at Charleston.

The above information was compiled from the book *Atlantic Hurricanes* by
Gorden E. Dunn and Banner I. Miller (Louisiana State University Press, 1960)
and from reports in the Charleston *Courier* and the *South Carolina Gazette*.

4
Batteries & Fortifications
In the harbor, at Mount Pleasant
& on Sullivan's Island

BATTERY BEAUREGARD – Built by Confederate forces during 1862–63 on Sullivan's Island near the middle section of the island, it had an armament of one 10-inch Columbiad smoothbore, one 8-inch Columbiad rifled and banded, three 8-inch seacoast howitzers, three 32-pounders rifled and banded, two 24-pounders rifled and banded, one 6-pounder smoothbore, and one 6-pounder rifled.

BATTERY BEE – Built by Confederate forces in 1862 on the western end of Sullivan's Island, it had an armament of 11 cannon and mortars. The battery was blown up on February 18, 1865.

BATTERY BINGHAM – Located within Fort Moultrie proper, this battery was built in 1897 and had an armament of two 4.7-inch British Armstrong rapid-fire guns.

BATTERIES BUTLER and CAPRON – The "hill" fort on Sullivan's Island off Middle Street at Station 19. Built in 1898–99, it was originally designed as one battery to hold 16 12-inch mortars; in 1906, it was divided into two batteries of 8 12-inch mortars.

BATTERY GADSDEN – On Sullivan's Island at Station 19, it was built in 1906 as part of the Endicott defenses of Charleston harbor and had an armament of four 6-inchers on pedestal mounts.

BATTERY GARY – Built by Confederate forces at Mount Pleasant overlooking the harbor and Cove Inlet. Its armament consisted of two 8-inch rifles. A small battery was also located here during the Revolutionary War.

BATTERY HUGER – Located within Fort Sumter proper, it was built in 1899 as part of the Endicott defenses of Charleston harbor and had an armament of two 12-inch rifles.

BATTERY JASPER – Built in 1897–98 as part of the Endicott defenses of Charleston harbor, this battery is located just to the east of Fort Moultrie, and had four 10-inch disappearing rifles, with a capability of firing 571-pound projectiles more than 8 miles.

BATTERY LOGAN – Located on Sullivan's Island, just past Battery Jasper, and built in 1897–98 as part of the Endicott defenses of Charleston harbor, it had an armament of one 6-inch barbette rifle and one 6-inch disappearing rifle.

BATTERY McCORKLE – Located within Fort Moultrie proper, it was built in 1899 and had an armament of three rapid-fire 15-pounders.

BATTERY MARSHALL – Built by Confederate forces at the north end of Sullivan's Island at Breach Inlet in 1863, on or near the site of a Revolutionary War battery. It had an armament of 14 various-calibered smoothbores, rifles, and howitzers. Fort Marshall, officially called Construction 520, was erected here in 1943, with an armament of two 12-inch Model 1895-M1 guns en barbette carriages, set 420 feet apart, and sited to allow each of the two guns a field of fire of 145 degrees. Although they were never used in combat, they had the capacity of firing a 975-pound projectile 29,300 yards, with each gun capable of firing one-and-a-half rounds per minute.

BATTERY THOMPSON – On Sullivan's Island at Station 19, it was built in 1906 as part of the Endicott defense system for Charleston harbor and had an armament of two 10-inch disappearing rifles.

BEACH BATTERIES – Small batteries erected by Confederate forces during the Civil war on the Mount Pleasant seacoast mainland; one was located at Kinloch's Landing and another at Venning's Landing, both guarding the creeks at Copahee Sound.

CASTLE PINCKNEY – Located in Charleston harbor on Shute's Folly, the first fortification was a horseshoe battery erected in 1742. A second wooden structure made of palisades and sand was destroyed by the hurricane of 1804. Rebuilt of brick, it was the most important fortification in the harbor during the War of 1812. During the Civil War, the Confederates used it as a place to hold Federal prisoners taken at the first Battle of Manassas (Bull Run). It was used as a light station until 1917.

FORT MOULTRIE – It was originally built in 1776 as Fort Sullivan. There have been three Fort Moultries at the same site. The first was built of palmetto logs and sand under the command of Colonel (later General) William Moultrie. This fort was washed away by the hurricane of 1783. A second fort, built in 1796–98, was a five-sided enclosed fort, surrounded by an 8-foot ditch in which six English 12-pounder cannon were positioned, along with a well and shot furnace. Inside the fort were ten French 26-pounders. This fort was almost completely destroyed by the hurricane of 1804. The third Fort Moultrie was begun in 1808 and is the fort that remains today. The fort was strengthened during the War of 1812 and the Civil War, and by 1860, it had an armament of over 50 cannon, including 19 32-pounders, 16 24-pounders, 10 8-inch columbiads, 6 howitzers, 4 bronze 6-pounders, and a 10-inch mortar. It was severely damaged during the Civil War, and renovations on Fort Moultrie were finally completed in 1876, with two 15-inch Rodmans and two 200-pounder Parrotts mounted inside the fort and four 13-inch mortars erected to the north of the fort. In the late 1800s and early 1900s, Fort Moultrie was modernized again as part of the Endicott system of coastal defenses, and additional batteries were built across Sullivan's Island. During World War I, Fort Moultrie had barracks for 3,000 men. In the period between the World Wars, Fort Moultrie grew as a major training area for the National Guard and the Citizens Military Training Camp, with an average of 600 youths arriving each summer for a month of intensive military training. During World War II, Fort Moultrie was again modernized, adding new batteries of heavy artillery surrounded with a shell of reinforced concrete and earth. Also Construction 520 (Fort Marshall) was built at Breach Inlet. Deactivated in 1947, Fort Moultrie became part of the National Park Service in 1960.

FORT PLEASANT – Fortified during the Revolutionary War by the Americans, it was later occupied by British troops on April 25, 1780, and used as a prisoner-of-war encampment for American officers.

FORT RIPLEY – Built in 1862 by Confederate forces on a shoal in the harbor just off the tip of the Charleston peninsula, this small fort was built on a crib work of pine and palmetto logs and used as a signal station.

FORT SUMTER – Built on a sandbar in the center of the entrance to Charleston harbor, Fort Sumter was begun in 1829. It took almost 15 years and thousands of tons of granite just to build the foundation, and it wasn't until the mid-1840s that construction on the fort, itself, could begin. By 1860 and some 7 million bricks later, the five-sided, three-tiered fort stood 50 feet above the water. Designed to hold 135 guns, it was still only 90 percent complete at the outset of the Civil War, when it was initially held by a garrison of 85 officers and men under Major Robert Anderson. After two days of steady bombardment, on April 13, 1861, Anderson surrendered the fort to the Confederates, who held the fort until February 17, 1865, when Charleston fell to Union troops. The fort was all but demolished during this war, and it wasn't until the 1870s that repairs were made and the fort rearmed. In 1898, Battery Huger was built within the fort, a reinforced concrete fortification with an armament of 12-inch breech-loading guns. The fort remained in active service until the close of World War II.

The Battle of Fort Sullivan
June 28, 1776

Fort Sullivan was a small, uncompleted, crudely built fort made of palmetto logs and sand, which had been called a "slaughter pen" by General Charles Lee, commander of American forces, when the British fleet attacked Sullivan's Island on June 28, 1776. Under Admiral Peter Parker, more than 50 British support vessels and men-of-war were anchored at Five Fathom Hole off Morris Island. Approximately 2,500 officers and soldiers under Major General Henry Clinton were encamped on Long Island (now Isle of Palms), prepared to cross Breach Inlet, and invade Sullivan's Island from the north. The garrison at Fort Sullivan had an incredibly meager armament, consisting of a hurriedly found assortment of cannon ranging from 9- and 12-pounders to French 26-pounders, with precious little ammunition. Colonel William Thompson's "Advance Guard," consisting of only 300 sharpshooters and 2 cannon, were placed on the northern end of Sullivan's Island to stop the invading land forces at Breach Inlet. To the Briton's 32,000 pounds of powder, the Americans had less than 5,000 pounds.

It was against these tremendous odds that Colonel William Moultrie faced the enemy. At 9 a.m. on June 28th, Parker began to maneuver his men-of-war with their complement of nearly 300 heavy guns into place. The *Thunder* and *Friendship* anchored about a mile and a half from the fort, while the *Bristol, Experiment, Active,* and *Solebay* took positions in a line approximately 400 yards from the fort. At 11:30 a.m., the *Thunder* began lofting 13-inch mortars at the fort. Moultrie's men returned fire on the *Active*, hitting her several times. Then came the powerful barrage from the British broadsides, allowing the frigates *Sphinx, Syren,* and *Actæon* to move in towards the Cove and attack the fort from the rear.

Prior to the battle, John Rutledge, president of South Carolina's revolutionary government, had given Moultrie a final order: "Be cool and do mischief." As the battle wore on, despite constant and heavy British fire, Moultrie fired his cannon as infrequently as possible, preserving his powder. The fort was taking a terrible beating, but the damage was not as bad as expected since the fort's walls of palmetto logs were literally accepting the British projectiles like a sponge and the sand was successfully smothering most of the bombs before they could explode. Parker pulled his men-of-war in closer, assuming the small fort was close to surrender. Moultrie then opened a steady, deliberate fire.

By 9:00 p.m., Parker was forced to retreat. The *Bristol* had been hit 70 times and had 40 dead, with 71 wounded. The *Experiment* had 23 dead and 56 wounded. The *Active* and the *Solebay* suffered 15 casualties. Unfamiliar with the sandbars at the south end of the island, the *Actæon*, *Sphinx*, and *Syren* were hard aground, with the *Actæon* in flames.

Clinton's forces at Breach Inlet had been even less successful. Thompson's sharpshooters raked the advancing British, and as North Carolinian Morgan Brown related later: "Our rifles were in prime order, well proved and well charged; every man took deliberate aim at his object . . . The fire taught the enemy to lie closer behind their bank of oyster shells, and only show themselves when they rose up to fire."

This remarkable American victory kept the British from invading Charleston for four years. Moultrie was not only promoted to general but, to honor his valor, the fort was renamed Fort Moultrie.

Bibliography

"A Bill of Complaint in Chancery, 1700." *South Carolina Historical Magazine*, Volume 22 (1921).

Archaeological Survey of the Seaside Farms Tract. Chicora Foundation Research Series 35.

Audubon, Marie R. *Audubon and His Journals*. New York: Charles Scribner's Sons, 1899.

Baldwin, Agnes Leland. *First Settlers of South Carolina 1670–1680*. Columbia: South Carolina Tricentennial Commission.

Barnwell, Joseph W. "Letters of John Rutledge." *South Carolina Historical Magazine*, Volume 18 (1917).

Batson, Wade T. *Wildflowers in the Carolinas*. Columbia: University of South Carolina Press, 1987.

Benjamin, S.G.W. "The Sea Islands." *Harpers Magazine*, 1878.

Berkeley, Edmund, and Dorothy Smith. *The Life and Travels of John Bartram*. Tallahassee: Florida State University, 1982.

Biographical Directory of the South Carolina House of Representatives, Volume II and III. Walter B. Edgar and N. Louise Baily, eds. Columbia: University of South Carolina Press, 1977.

Birds of the Carolinas. Eloise F. Potter, James F. Parnell, and Robert P. Teulings, eds. Chapel Hill: University of North Carolina Press, 1980.

Brewster, Lawrence F. *Summer Migrations and Resorts of South Carolina Lowcountry Planters*. Durham: Duke University Press, 1947.

Bulger, William T. "Sir Henry Clinton's Journal of the Siege of Charleston, 1780." *South Carolina Historical Magazine*, Volume 66 (1965).

Carroll, B.R. *Historical Collections of South Carolina, Volumes I and II*. New York: Harper & Brothers, 1836.

"Castle Pinckney: An Archaeological Assessment with Recommendations." Kenneth E. Lewis and William Langhorne Jr., eds. University of South Carolina: Institute of Archeology and Anthropology, 1978.

Catesby, Mark. *The Natural History of Carolina, Florida & the Bahama Islands*. London, 1731.

Clark, Thomas D. *South Carolina, the Grand Tour 1780–1865*. Columbia: University of South Carolina Press, 1973.

Clifton, James M. "The Rice Driver: His Role in Slave Management." *South Carolina Historical Magazine*, Volume 82 (1981).

Clute, Robert C. *The Annals and Parish Register of St. Thomas and St. Denis Parish from 1680–1884*. Charleston Library Society, APm Series 6, No. 4.

Cooper, Thomas, M.D. *The Statutes at Large of South Carolina*. Columbia, 1838.

"Cultural Resources Inventory of the Sewee Golf Club Tract." Eric C. Poplin, Harry Pecorelli III, and Bruce G. Harvey, eds. Brockington & Associates, Inc., 1999.

Cronise, Florence M., and Henry W. Ward. *Cunnie Rabbit, Mr. Spider and the Other Beef*. New York: E.P. Dutton & Co., 1903.

Dalcho, Frederick. *An Historical Account of the Protestant Episcopal Church in South Carolina*. Charleston: E. Thayer, 1820.

Doar, David. "An Address given to the Agricultural Society of St. James Santee, July 4, 1908." Charleston Calder-Fladger Co., 1908.

— *Rice and Rice Planting in the South Carolina Lowcountry*. Charleston Museum, 1936.

Drayton, John. *A View of South-Carolina as Respects her Natural and Civil Concerns*. Charleston: W.P. Young, 1802.

Edgar, Walter. *South Carolina: A History*. Columbia: University of South Carolina Press, 1998.

Edwards, George N. *A History of the Independent or Congregational Church of Charleston*. Boston, 1947.

Feduccia, Alan. *Catesby's Birds of Colonial America*. Chapel Hill & London: University of North Carolina Press, 1985.

Fleetwood, William C. Jr. *Tidecraft: The Boats of South Carolina, Georgia and Northeastern Florida, 1550–1950*. Georgia: WBG Marine Press, 1995.

Ford, Alice. *John James Audubon, A Biography*. New York: Abbeville Press, 1988.

Fortescue, J.W. *Calendar of State Papers, Colonial Series, America & West Indies, 1681–1685*. London: Eyre & Spottiswoode, 1898.

Furnas, J.C. *The Americans: A Social History of the United States, 1587–1914*. New York: G.P. Putnam's Sons, 1969.

"Fundamental Constitutions of Carolina." *South Carolina Historical Magazine*, Volume 71 (1970).

Gibbes, Robert W., M.D. *Documentary History of the American Revolution*. New York: D. Appleton & Co., 1857.

Gregorie, Anne King. *Notes on Seewee Indians and Indian Remains of Christ Church Parish*. Charleston Museum, 1928.

— *Christ Church, 1706–1769, A Plantation Parish of the South Carolina Establishment*. Charleston, S.C.: Dalcho Historical Society, 1961.

Haskell, John Bachman. *John Bachman*. Charleston: Walker, Evans & Cogswell Co., 1888.

Hicks, Theresa M. *South Carolina Indians, Indian Transactions and Other Ethnic Connections, Beginning in 1670*. Spartanburg: The Reprint Company, 1998.

Howe, Reverend George. *History of the Presbyterian Church in South Carolina*. Columbia: Duffie & Chapman, 1870.

Hudson, Charles. *The Juan Pardo Expeditions: Exploration of the Carolinas and Tennessee, 1566–68*. Washington: Smithsonian Institute Press, 1990.

— *The Southeastern Indians*. Knoxville: University of Tennessee Press, 1976.

Irving, John B. *A Day on Cooper River*. Louisa Cheves Stoney, ed. Columbia: R.L. Bryan Company, 1969.

Ivers, Larry. "Scouting the Inland Passages, 1685–1737." *South Carolina Historical Magazine*, Volume 73 (1972).

Jacoby, Mary Moore, ed. with George C. Rogers Jr. *The Churches of Charleston and the Lowcountry*. Columbia: University of South Carolina Press, 1994.

Jones, George Fenwick. "John Martin Boltzius' Trip to Charleston, October 1742." *South Carolina Historical Magazine*, Volume 82 (1981).

Johnson, John. *The Defence of Charleston Harbor, including Fort Sumter and the Adjacent Islands, 1863–65*. Charleston: Walker Evans & Cogswell, 1890.

Klingberg, Frank J. *Carolina Chronicle, The Papers of Commissary Gideon Johnston, 1707–1716*. Berkeley and Los Angeles: University of California Press, 1946.

Langley, Lynne. *Nature Watch in the Carolina Lowcountry*. Charleston: News & Courier and Evening Post Publishing Co., 1987.

Lawson, John. *A Voyage to Carolina Containing the Exact Description and Natural History of that County, Together with the Present State thereof and a Journal of a Thousand Miles, Travel'd thro' several Nations of Indians, Giving a Particular Account of their Customs, Manners, &c.* London: 1709.

Leiding, Harriette Kershaw. *Historic Houses of South Carolina*. New York and Philadelphia: J.P. Lippincott Company, 1921.

Littlefield, Daniel C. *Rice and Slaves, Ethnicity and the Slave Trade in Colonial South Carolina*. Baton Rouge and London: Louisiana State University Press, 1981.

Mammals of the Carolinas, Virginia and Maryland. Wm. David Webster, James F. Parnell, and Walter C. Biggs Jr., eds. Chapel Hill & London: University of North Carolina Press, 1985.

Mathews, Maurice. "A Contemporary View of Carolina in 1680." *South Carolina Historical Magazine*, Volume 55 (1954).

McCormick, JoAnn. *The Quakers of Colonial South Carolina 1670–1807*. Ph.D. Thesis. University of South Carolina, 1984.

McIver, Petrona Royall. "Wappetaw Congregational Church." *South Carolina Historical Magazine*, Volume 58 (1957).

Merrins, H. Roy. "The Journal of Ebenezer Hazard." *South Carolina Historical Magazine*, Volume 73 (1972).

Meyer, Peter. *Nature Guide to the Carolina Coast*, Wilmington: Avian Cetecean Press, 1992.

Milling, Chapman J. *Red Carolinians*. Columbia: University of South Carolina Press, 1940.

Mills, Robert. *Statistics of South Carolina, including a View of its Natural, Civil and Military History, General and Particular*. Charleston: Hurlbut and Lloyd, 1826.

Moore, Caroline T., and Agatha Aimar Simmons. *Abstracts of the Wills of the State of South Carolina, 1670–1740*. Columbia: R.L. Bryan Company, 1960.

Orvin, Maxwell Clayton. *Historic Berkeley County, 1671–1900*. Charleston, 1973.

Peckham, Howard H. *Narratives of Colonial America, 1704–1765*. Chicago: The Lakeside Press, R.B. Donnelly & Sons Company, 1971.

McIver, Petrona Royall. *History of Mount Pleasant, S.C.* Charleston: 1960.

— "Early Taverns on the Georgetown Road." *Names in South Carolina*, Volume 14 (1913).

— "Wappetaw Congregational Church." *South Carolina Historical Magazine*, Volume 58 (1957); also Volume 71 (1970).

Moultrie, William. *Memoirs of the American Revolution*. New York: David Longworth, 1802.

Murray, Chalmers S. *This Our Land*. Charleston: South Carolina Art Association, 1949.

Neuffer, Claude Henry. *The Christopher Happoldt Journal, His European Tour with Rev. John Bachman*. The Charleston Museum, 1960.

Hudson, Charles. *The Southeastern Indians*. Knoxville: The University of Tennessee Press, 1976.

Opala, Joseph A. *The Gullah*. Freetown, Sierra Leone, 1987.

Palmer, Colin. "African Slave Trade, the Cruelest Commerce." *National Geographic Magazine*, September 1992, Vol. 182, No. 3.

The Papers of Henry Laurens (1747–1788). Vol. 1–13. Philip M. Hamer, George Rogers, David R. Chesnutt, and C. James Taylor, eds. Columbia: University of South Carolina Press, 1968–1991.

Poyas, Elizabeth Anne. *Shadows of the Past, By the Ancient Lady*. Charleston: Wm. M. Mazyck, 1870.

Ramsay, Dr. David. *History of South Carolina*. Newberry: W.D. Duffie, 1858.

Ravenel, Dr. Edmund. *The Advantages of a Sea-Shore Resident in the Treatment of Certain Diseases and the Therapeutic Employment of Sea-Water*. Charleston: Walker & James, 1850.

Reiger, George. *Wanderer on My Native Shore*. New York: Simon and Schuster, 1983.

Rivers, William James. *A Sketch of the History of South Carolina*. Charleston: 1874.

Robbins, Walter L. "John Tobler's Description of South Carolina, 1754." *South Carolina Historical Magazine*, Volume 71 (1970).

Rogers, George C. Jr. *Charleston in the Age of the Pinckneys*. Columbia: University of South Carolina Press, 1969.

Rosen, Robert N. *A Short History of Charleston*. San Francisco: LEXIKOS, 1982.

Royall, Mary-Julia C. *Mount Pleasant: The Victorian Village*. Charleston: Arcadia Publishing, 1997.

— *Mount Pleasant: The Friendly Town*. Charleston: Arcadia Publishing, 2002.

Rural Settlement in the Charleston Bay Area: 18th and 19th Century Sites in the Mark Clark Expressway Corridor. Paul Brockington, Michael Scardaville, Patrick H. Garrow, David Singer, Linda France, and Cheryl Hott, eds. Columbia: Department of Highway & Public Transportation, 1985.

Salley, Alexander S. *The Early English Settlers of South Carolina*. Printed for The National Society of the Colonial Dames of America in the State of South Carolina, 1946.

— *Journals of the Grand Council, 1671–1681*. Historical Commission of South Carolina, 1907.

— "Journal of General Peter Horry." *South Carolina Historical Magazine*, Volume 40 (1939).

— *Narratives of Early Carolina 1670–1708*. New York: Charles Scribner's Sons, 1911.

— *Warrants for Land in South Carolina*. Historical Commission of South Carolina, 1910.

Sharrer, G. Terry. "Indigo in Carolina, 1671–1796." *South Carolina Historical Magazine*, Volume 72 (1971).

Smith, Henry A.M. *The Baronies of South Carolina*. South Carolina Historical Society, 1931.

— "Old Charles Town and Its Vicinity, Accabee and Wappoo Where Indigo was First Cultivated, with Some Adjoining Places in Old St. Andrews Parish." *South Carolina Historical Magazine*, Volume 16 (1915).

— "Some Forgotten Towns in Lower South Carolina." *South Carolina Historical Magazine*, Volume 14 (1913).

— "The Orange Quarter and the First French Settlers in South Carolina." *South Carolina Historical Magazine*, Volume 18 (1917).

Smith, W. Roy. *South Carolina as a Royal Province*. New York: MacMillan Company, 1903.

Smith, Warren B. *White Servitude in Colonial South Carolina*. Columbia: University of South Carolina Press, 1961.

Snell, William Robert. *Indian Slavery in Colonial South Carolina*. Ph.D. Dissertation. The University of Alabama, 1972.

Staudenraus, P.J. "Letters from South Carolina 1821–1822." *South Carolina Historical Magazine*, Volume 58 (1957).

Swanton, John R. *Indians of the Southeastern United States*. Washington: U.S. Government Printing Office, 1946.

— *Early History of the Creek Indians and Their Neighbors*. Washington: Smithsonian Institute, Bureau of Ethnology, U.S. Government Printing Office, 1922.

— *The Indian Tribes of North America*. Washington: U.S. Government Printing Office, 1953.

Thomas, John P. Jr. "The Barbadians in Early South Carolina." *South Carolina Historical Magazine*, Volume 31 (1930).

Tobler, John. "Description of South Carolina, 1753." *South Carolina Historical Magazine*, Volume 71 (1970).

Trinkley, Michael. "With Credit & Honor." Address on Seaside Plantation given to Mount Pleasant History Symposium, 1996.

— *A Historical & Archaeological Evaluation of the Elfe & Sanders Plantations*. Chicora Foundation, 1985.

Twining, Mary Arnold. *An Examination of African Retentions in the Folk Culture of the South Carolina and Georgia Sea Islands*. Ph.D. Thesis. Indiana University, 1977.

Verner, Elizabeth O'Neill. *Mellowed by Time*. Columbia: Bostick & Thornley, Inc., 1941.

Waddell, Gene. *Charleston in 1883*. Easley: Southern Historical Press, 1983.

— *Indians of the South Carolina Lowcountry*. Columbia: University of South Carolina Press, 1980.

Wallace, David Duncan. *South Carolina: A Short History*. Chapel Hill: University of North Carolina Press, 1951.

Waring, Joseph. *A History of Medicine In South Carolina, 1670–1825*. Charleston: South Carolina Medical Association, 1964.

Wayne, Lucy B. "Burning Brick: A Study of a Lowcountry Industry." Ph.D. Thesis. University of Florida, 1992.

Webber, Mabel L. "The Register of Christ Church Parish." *South Carolina Historical Magazine*, Volumes 18–21.

— "Extracts from the Journal of Mrs. Ann Manigault, 1754–1781." *South Carolina Historical Magazine*, Volume 20 (1919).

— "Josiah Smith's Diary, 1780–81." *South Carolina Historical Magazine*, Volume 31, 32, 33 (1930, 1931, 1932).

Wood, Peter H. *Black Majority, Negroes in Colonial South Carolina, From 1670 through the Stono Rebellion*. New York: Alfred A. Knopf, 1974.

Index

Atamasco Lily 84
Atlanticville 20, 109
Atlantic Beach Hotel 20,
    84
Atlantic Coast Hurricane
    of 1830 125
Atlantic Coast Hurricane
    of 1839 125
Atlantic Wharf 83
Audubon, John James
    15, 20, 21, 24, 34, 44,
    95, 96
Audubon Society 21
Augusta, Georgia 32
Austin, George 71
Austin & Laurens 71
Avendaugh-bough 21
Aviles, Pedro Mendendez
    de 88
Avignnon, France 86
Awendaw 12, 21, 22, 67,
    71, 76, 100, 101, 103,
    104, 118
Awendaw Barony 103
Awendaw Creek 21, 39,
    101, 103
Axson, R. K. 100

B

Bachman, Dr. John 21,
    95, 96
Bachman Sparrow 21
Bachman Warbler 21
Back River 115
Bahai de Cayagua 21
Bahamas 93
Bald Eagle 21
Ball, Captain 43
Ball, Eleanor (Mrs. Henry
    Laurens) 71
Ball, Elias 58, 73
Ball, John 70

Ball, John Sr. 65
Ball, William 59
Ball, William J. 24
Balloon Hoax, The 92
Ball family 42, 59, 70,
    73, 94
Bandstand 21
Barbados 12, 13, 18, 22,
    24, 28, 33, 38, 41, 46,
    47, 55, 63, 94
Barksdale's Point 84, 86
Barksdale, Elizabeth
    (Mrs. Andrew Hibben)
    22
Barksdale, John 21, 22
Barony 22
Barrier Islands 9, 12,
    22, 31, 33, 35, 40, 47,
    65, 66, 68, 71, 86, 91,
    102, 109, 112, 113
Bartlam, John 23
Bartram, John 23
Bartram, William 23,
    107
Bassford, James 74
Bath, North Carolina 26
Batteries & Fortifications
    23, 39, 53, 68, 77, 81
Batteries Butler & Cap-
    ron 129
Battery, the 23, 28
Battery Beauregard 23,
    129
Battery Bee 129
Battery Bingham 129
Battery Gadsden 129
Battery Gary 38, 130
Battery Huger 53, 130,
    132
Battery Jasper 68, 130
Battery Logan 130
Battery Marshall 65, 77,
    130

Battery McCorkle 130
Battery Thompson 130
Battery Wagner 39
Battle of Savannah 68
Baxter, Edward 18
Bayberry 33
Beach Batteries 130
Beach Channel 110
Beale's wharf 110
Beaufort 12
Beauregard, General
    Pierre G.T. 23
Bedonis Alley 57
Beecher, James Chaplin
    23, 70, 73
Beehive 24
Bee family 24
Belin family 29
Bell, John 62
Bellinger, Edmund 61,
    72
Belvue-Bermuda Planta-
    tion 24, 25, 74, 114
Benison, George 121
Bennett, Thomas 30
Ben Sawyer Boulevard
    36, 78, 99
Ben Sawyer Bridge 66
Beresford, Mary 78
Beresford, Richard 24,
    25
Beresford, Richard Jr. 24,
    25, 40, 75
Beresford Bounty 24
Beresford Bounty Planta-
    tion 24, 32
Beresford Creek 17, 25,
    46, 68, 119
Beresford Hall 24, 25
Berkeley, John 74
Berkeley, William 74
Berkeley, William and
    John 25

H

X